SECRETS OF CHURCHILL'S WAR ROOMS

Published by IWM, Lambeth Road, London SE1 6HZ
iwm.org.uk

ISBN 978-1-904897-49-1

A catalogue record for this book is
available from the British Library.
Printed and bound by Gomer Press Limited

Every effort has been made to contact all copyright
holders. The publishers will be glad to make good
in future editions any error or omissions brought
to their attention.

SECRETS OF CHURCHILL'S WAR ROOMS

Jonathan Asbury

CONTENTS

INTRODUCTION

Churchill didn't enjoy using his War Rooms. When enemy bombs began to drop over London, his natural instinct was to head up the nearest staircase rather than down, seeking out a vantage point from which to watch the action. He is known to have slept in his underground bedroom only a handful of times, and it is thought that he may never have eaten in the dining room set aside for his personal use.

Nonetheless, Churchill was immensely proud of his underground complex. He took great pleasure in showing it off to visiting generals and statesmen, and was particularly fond of the Map Room. Here he could often be found watching the results of his decisions playing out on the charts hung around the walls. He even took an active interest in the fabric of the building, ordering the installation of defensive structures to protect it against bomb blasts, and insisting on making regular torch-lit inspections of progress, clambering over traverses and, on one occasion, soaking his shoes in liquid cement.

While those accidental footprints may not have been preserved for posterity, there are many other tell-tale signs of Churchill's presence throughout the rooms. The microphone on his desk conjures up the trenchant words that he broadcast to the nation from here in the dark days of 1940. His insistence on fast, efficient decision-making survives in the 'Action This Day' labels he invented to mark the most urgent documents. The tension he felt during War Cabinet meetings is still visible decades later in the deep scratch marks he gouged in the arms of his chair.

Those scratch marks give evidence to the fact that, like it or not, Churchill spent a good deal of time locked away in the War Rooms – especially in the months immediately after he became Prime Minister in May 1940, when the possibility of German invasion loomed, the Battle of Britain raged and, in September, the nightly bombing of London began.

War Rooms staff remember how he used to prowl the corridors in the dead of night 'studying things in his mind', pausing every now and then to peer over the shoulder of one of the typists labouring away at a hastily arranged alcove desk. At other times his bulky frame could be found lying across his bed 'looking…not totally proper' as he dictated a speech to his secretary, or his presence would be announced by a bang on the pipes, warning staff to keep down the noise as he grabbed one of his famous afternoon naps. Even when he was thousands of miles away from Whitehall on

Winston Churchill at his seat in the Cabinet Room at No 10 Downing Street, London, 1940

one of his many overseas trips, staff recall that the atmosphere and culture of the place owed much to Churchill's animating energy.

Indeed, if Churchill is often seen as the embodiment of – and inspiration for – Britain's steadfast wartime resolution and indefatigable spirit, the War Rooms capture the same qualities in bricks and mortar. Both stand testament to one of the key elements in Britain's eventual triumph – the capacity for brilliant

improvisation in the face of deadly necessity. Where else but in Churchill's War Rooms, for example, would one of the most secret communication facilities in the world be kept concealed by the simple addition of a lavatory-style lock on the door?

There have been innumerable accounts of Churchill's role in the Second World War, and also some excellent publications looking at the story of the War Rooms, drawing heavily on the painstaking research undertaken by IWM's historians as they set about their extraordinary preservation and restoration of the site. This book, however, was conceived to perform a slightly different role – to weave together the parallel stories of Churchill and his War Rooms, showing when, how and why Britain's bulldog prime minister made use of them, and explaining his continual reliance on the work that was done there. In so doing, it owes an enormous debt to all those many works of history that precede it.

Taking readers behind the glass screens of the modern-day museum, the book picks out objects and views that not only reveal something about the function of the rooms, but also give an insight into what it was like to work there. In that sense, the book is not only about Churchill and his War Rooms, but also about his War Rooms staff – the remarkable men and women, military and civilian, young and old who worked, ate and slept there in pursuit of survival and, ultimately, victory. It is only by drawing on their first-hand experiences – committed to paper in memoirs, letters and diaries, or related to IWM historians in specially recorded interviews – that the secrets of Churchill's War Rooms can truly be revealed. This book is dedicated to them.

1

THE THREAT AND SHOCK OF WAR

July 1936 to May 1940

On 28 July 1936, backbench MP Winston Churchill stood up to address Prime Minister Stanley Baldwin in a private room at the House of Commons. He had called for the meeting himself, concerned that the government was not doing enough to meet the military threat posed by a resurgent Germany – especially from the air. For an hour and a quarter he laid out his position, and towards the end he posed a question:

> Have we organised and created an alternative centre of government if London is thrown into confusion? No doubt there has been some discussion of this on paper, but has anything been done to provide one or two alternative centres of command, with adequate deep-laid telephone connections and wireless, from which the necessary orders can be given by some coherent thinking-mechanism?

He was talking about the creation of a 'War Room', and the fact was that the government had taken no practical steps in that direction at all.

Churchill himself was partly to blame. After the First World War the British government adopted a 'ten-year rule', instructing every department to operate on the assumption that the country would not go to war again for at least a decade. In 1928, when this ten-year period was coming to an end, Churchill was Chancellor of the Exchequer for the Conservative government, tasked with finding ways to save money. He proposed that the ten-year rule be continually reset, so that the possibility of Britain going to war would forever be pushed a decade into the future. This allowed him to curb defence spending, with the result that little was done to prepare for a future war.

The following year, the Conservatives were voted out of office, and by the time they regained power in 1931 Churchill had fallen out of favour with the party leadership – in particular over the question of Indian Home Rule. The government wanted to grant India the status of a dominion; Churchill did not. For the next four years he argued his case stridently in Parliament, becoming further and further estranged from the party. By 1935, when the government's bill was passed with a resounding majority, Churchill was over 60 years old. He was starting to look like yesterday's man.

In January 1933, the Nazi Party's Adolf Hitler came to power in Germany. In October that year he shocked the world by announcing his country's withdrawal from the League of Nations. His stated reason was simple:

it was no longer acceptable for the Western powers to stop Germany from gaining military parity. Germany was set on rearming itself. The chances of war in the next decade were suddenly much higher.

Baldwin decided that the best way to ensure peace was for all sides to commit to disarmament. Churchill, on the other hand, called for Britain to build up its armed forces – not because he would welcome a war, but because he thought that military strength could act as a deterrent as well as an insurance policy.

It was a campaign that he conducted with customary vigour, and which did nothing to reconcile him to the government or to the wider public, who had little appetite for a new war with Germany. 'Germany is arming – she is rapidly arming – and no-one will stop her,' he called out from the back benches, but he was dismissed as 'alarmist' by Prime Minister and newspapers alike.

Several months after Churchill's meeting with Baldwin, the government still had no firm plan from where it would run the next war in the event of a German air attack. As Churchill had suspected, there had been plenty of discussion on paper – one suggestion was for key personnel to be evacuated to the suburbs or out into the West Country – but there had been little or no action.

The idea of a 'war room' in itself was not a new one; it had long been assumed, for example, that each of the three armed services would have one of its own. But what Churchill was asking was how the work of the armed services would be co-ordinated, and crucially how the connection between the government and its fighting forces could be protected.

The dangers of the status quo were revealed in late 1937 when air defence exercises highlighted all sorts of confusion between the armed services. Now, at last, there was talk of a 'combined war room' to house the heads of the Army, Navy and Air Force (known as the Chiefs of Staff), the Deputy Chiefs of Staff and the Joint Planners, whose job it was to assess the military situation and devise suitable strategies.

In response to a request from the Deputy Chiefs, staff at the Air Ministry drew up an elaborate plan for a fully protected, purpose-built underground war room, which could be located in the basement of a new building being planned in Whitehall. This was all very well – in fact the plan was approved on 24 March 1938 – but the reality was that such a building would take at least four years to complete.

Colonel Hastings Ismay wasn't prepared to wait that long. As Deputy Secretary of Britain's Committee of Imperial Defence – a body set up in 1902 to research and advise on matters of military strategy – he was more aware than most of how loudly the clock was ticking. On the morning of 12 March 1938, Hitler had sent his troops into Austria to enforce its incorporation into Nazi Germany. International tensions were soaring, and Ismay could all too easily imagine a German attack on Britain long before any purpose-built war room could be completed.

On 16 March he took matters into his own hands, asking the Office of Works to search for a refuge where the War Cabinet and Chiefs of Staff could carry out their duties in case of emergency. This was the first practical step in the creation of what we now know as Churchill War Rooms. It was also the first time that anyone had suggested housing Britain's political and military leaders in the same facility. In fact it was only on 4 May 1938 that the Deputy Chiefs of Staff agreed to the idea.

With plans still in this confused and evolving state, news in late May that German troops were massing on the Czechoslovakian border was especially alarming. There might be war any day, but still no war room.

Ismay pressed on with renewed determination. After a rapid survey of available London basements, the Office of Works concluded that the most suitable was underneath the western end of the New Public Offices on Great George Street – conveniently close to Downing Street and Parliament. On 31 May 1938 the site was confirmed. The Chiefs of Staff gave Ismay free rein to create an 'emergency war headquarters' and ordered the Joint Planners to help him.

Right from the start, it was understood that this was just a temporary measure – only to be used if an emergency struck before a permanent war room could be built.

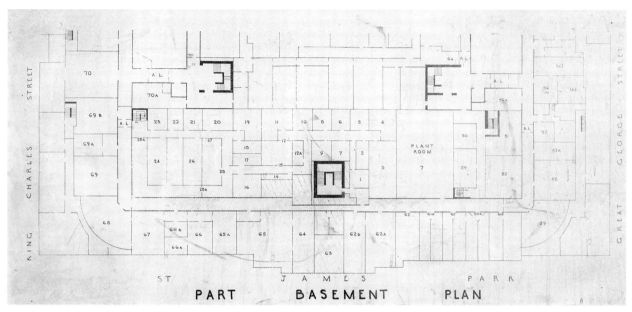

One of the original early plans for use of the basement

'Nothing very elaborate is contemplated,' Ismay informed the Treasury on 18 June; 'no major structural alterations, no air conditioning or costly gas proofing, and no expensive fittings.'

Ismay's first move was to delegate the day-to-day running of the project to his deputy, Brigadier Leslie Hollis. He in turn called on the help of colleague Lawrence Burgis, with further practical assistance from Eric de Normann of the Office of Works.

'Burgis and I had no precedent to work on,' recalled Hollis. 'This headquarters was to be the first of its type. For a week or two we pored over blueprints of the basement …and considered all the complex arrangements and requirements for which provision had to be made. Eventually we agreed on a plan.'

Over the next couple of months, Hollis, Burgis and de Normann presided over an extraordinary transformation under the streets of Whitehall. Rooms were cleared,

alcoves sandbagged, glass doors replaced with teak, brick partitions built, telephone lines installed – and a broadcasting connection was established by the BBC. It was a rapid, improvised process carried out to a brief that shifted constantly as events deteriorated on the Continent.

In September, for example, Hitler sparked a new crisis by threatening to annexe part of Czechoslovakia. Prime Minister Neville Chamberlain, who had taken over from Baldwin in May 1937, attempted to defuse the situation by diplomatic means but matters became so serious that, on 14 September, Ismay ordered that a ventilation system be fitted and made ready in the war rooms. He gave the workmen a week to complete the job. They managed it.

More work followed, including the gas proofing and air conditioning that Ismay had said would not be necessary. On 15 September came a request that the ceilings of the main rooms be strengthened with steel strutting. Two days later the request was extended to all the other rooms too. By 26 September the Central War Room, as the site was now known, was ready for emergency use and Ismay kept a set of keys with him at all times.

On 30 September the crisis on the Continent eased when Hitler signed the Munich Agreement and the Anglo-German Declaration, the latter declaring that Britain and Germany should never go to war with each other again. It was heralded by Chamberlain as a guarantee of 'peace for our time' but dismissed by Churchill as a 'defeat without a war'. Either way, the immediate danger appeared to have passed. The doors of the Central War Room were locked, and the exhausted staff of the Office of Works breathed a sigh of relief.

The Munich Agreement did not bring lasting peace, but it did provide valuable breathing space during which the Central War Room could be expanded and improved. In theory the facility was ready for use; indeed it had already been manned for a few days during the worst of the so-called Munich Crisis. Hollis had seen enough in that time to have grave concerns about using the rooms for real. The

Neville Chamberlain is greeted by Adolf Hitler at the Hotel Dreesen in Bad Godesberg, Germany, on 22 September 1938

ventilation system was poor, and there was no overnight accommodation, bedding, kitchen, food or washing facilities. Not for nothing did he and others refer to the facility as 'the hole in the ground', or simply 'the hole'.

For the first few months of 1939 Hollis battled unsuccessfully to convince the Office of Works to take action. As late as June the only toilets below ground in the Central War Room were of the 'sand and bucket variety' as one memo put it, and it was only in the last two weeks of August that chemical toilets and two dormitories were added.

The Office of Works carried out these improvements with a great deal of exasperation, frustrated that what had started out as a temporary facility was becoming something closer to semi-permanent. 'We have gone to a great deal of trouble and inconvenience in sacrificing this space,' they reported to Hollis, 'and we look to you to limit your requirements to what are absolutely essential, bearing in mind that the whole scheme is and must be of the nature of a makeshift...'

Makeshift or not, the chances of the Central War Room being used in earnest mounted throughout the summer. With German troops marching into Czechoslovakia in March 1939 tension rose again in Europe, and the officers who had been chosen to man the facility's Map Room were put on alert. A letter sent to Wing Commander John Heagerty, for example, asked him to be available 'at really short notice throughout August and September' and to 'let us know in advance of any intended absence from your normal address and telephone numbers, since it is impossible to foresee what may occur in Europe'.

Servicemen, politicians, press and public – all knew that it was now a question of when war would come rather than if. Churchill's stock had risen accordingly as his 'alarmist' predictions began to seem more prophetic. Twice, in November 1938, he had been granted the curious honour of being personally attacked by Hitler in speeches. This had prompted a natural reaction in his favour in the British press, and by the summer of 1939 the papers were full of clamour for him to return to the Cabinet.

On Wednesday 23 August Hitler signed a non-aggression pact with the Soviet Union, leaving Germany free to attack Poland – a country which Britain and France had pledged to support. Four days later, officers and staff made their way to the Central War Room, showed their passes to the Royal Marine guards, walked down the stairs to basement level and switched on the lights. It would be six years before these lights were turned off again.

Churchill was summoned out of the political wilderness and into Chamberlain's Cabinet on the afternoon of Friday 1 September, a dozen or so hours after Hitler's troops had invaded Poland. That same day, the Chiefs of Staff took to meeting in the Central War Room. They were in conference there at 11am on Sunday 3 September, when Ismay interrupted their meeting to tell them that the country was at war. They received the news without comment.

The Joint Planners were also at work in the Central War Room that Sunday morning. RAF Officer William Dickson recalls the first hour of the war very well:

> The PM announced that we were at war... [Radar] plots began to appear... enemy raids coming into this country... The sirens went over London... And then an extraordinary thing happened. The white telephone rang – the PM's personal telephone from No. 10... We'd briefed people on what to do when it did ring, but we never thought it would ring this early. It was the PM's secretary... the PM was due to make a speech in the House of Commons... was it safe for him to come out?

> I went into the Chiefs of Staff committee... and gave a brief description... Being splendidly British in every way they thanked me very much and... a couple of minutes later... it was all sorted out. Every single one of these raids was non-existent. It was something to do with switching on the radar.

Later that same day Churchill met with the Prime Minister to discuss what role he would take in the Cabinet. He was pleasantly surprised to be reappointed as First Lord of the Admiralty – a position he had occupied during the First World War. His brief, as political head of the Royal Navy, was to manage the conduct of the war at sea, which turned out to be where most of the action would be during the first few months of the conflict.

Churchill's first speech on returning to the front bench came on 26 September in a debate opened by the Prime Minister himself. According to Conservative MP and diarist Harold Nicolson, Chamberlain's address was uninspiring but Churchill set the chamber alight. 'He sounded every note from deep preoccupation to flippancy, from resolution to sheer boyishness. One could feel the spirits of the House rising with every word... In those twenty minutes Churchill brought himself nearer the post of Prime Minister than he has ever been before.'

Whether or not Churchill was destined for higher office, he certainly had no qualms about venturing beyond his brief at the Admiralty. He fired off memo after memo to Chamberlain on everything from the need to reshuffle the Cabinet to the detailed equipment of the Army in France. He also featured prominently in the minutes from War Cabinet meetings held during this period.

In the absence of air raids, Chamberlain held these meetings above ground at Downing Street or Parliament. Ismay, however, continued to insist on improvements to the Central War Room in case the situation changed. Before the end of September he asked for a bigger room to be made available for Cabinet meetings, forcing the Office of Works to give up a large chamber set aside as their own air raid shelter. By 4 October this room had been prepared and on 21 October it was decided to test it by holding a War Cabinet meeting.

Although it was the first time that Britain's political and military leaders had met in their underground facility, it was far from Churchill's first visit. He had already developed a strong interest in the work of the Map Room, making frequent visits to stay up to speed with events as details poured in from every theatre of the war.

By the time of that first meeting, the Central War Room was operational but overcrowded. Desks were continually being crammed into already occupied rooms, and partitions put up to turn one office into two. It remained unclear exactly what function this underground complex was supposed to perform – exacerbated perhaps by the fact that the War Cabinet hardly made use of the facility at all.

On 29 December 1939 the Cabinet Secretary Edward Bridges was moved to circulate a note stating that 'the Central War Room will in future be known as "the Cabinet War Room"'. Its function would be to maintain and supply 'an up to date general picture of the war in all parts of the world' for the War Cabinet, the Chiefs of Staff and the King, and to provide a 'protected meeting place for the War Cabinet and Chiefs of Staff organisation under air raid conditions'.

Underpinned by this new clarity of purpose, the Cabinet War Room entered 1940 in full working order, but the machinery of government itself was running less smoothly. At least three separate discussions had to be held before decisions could be reached on the most important issues – by the Chiefs of Staff, by the War Cabinet itself, and by a third body called the Committee for Military Co-ordination, set up to act as an intermediary between the two.

As a member of both the War Cabinet and the Military Co-ordination Committee, Churchill chafed at this inefficiency. In January 1940, he complained about the 'awful difficulties which our machinery of war-conduct presents to positive action', and continued: 'I see such immense walls of prevention, all built or building, that I wonder whether any plan will have a chance of climbing over them.'

He wrote as a prolific deviser of plans, schemes and stratagems. Since his restoration to the Admiralty he had advocated attacking Germany's western defences by land and air, dropping mines from aircraft into the Rhine to disrupt the country's main internal supply route, and cutting off German access to Swedish iron ore, which made its way to the country by sea via the Norwegian port of Narvik.

He pursued this last aim with dogged determination, first suggesting that neutral Norwegian waters be mined so that ships carrying iron ore would be forced out into the open sea where they could be sunk, then in late 1939 proposing an expedition to Narvik and an advance into Sweden to occupy the ore fields. But it wasn't until late March 1940 that the War Cabinet agreed to a mix of the two proposals: mining Norwegian waters and occupying Narvik.

Further delays meant that the mining operation didn't begin until 8 April, by which time the Germans were themselves landing in Norway to occupy Narvik. British attempts to dislodge them failed – a humiliating setback with echoes of the botched Gallipoli campaign in the First World War, which had also been advocated by Churchill. This time, however, it was clear to Whitehall insiders that Churchill was not to blame – that the campaign might in fact have proved successful had his advice been followed earlier.

A debate in Parliament on 7 May revealed widespread discontent with Chamberlain's leadership, prompting private discussions over the next two days between the beleaguered Prime Minister and his two potential successors, Churchill and the Foreign Minister Lord Halifax. Chamberlain's preferred candidate was Halifax, but as a peer he would have struggled to lead the government from the House of Lords. When he stepped aside, Churchill remained the only viable option.

Events on 10 May hurried the decision along. Hitler's armies launched a shock offensive in the Low Countries, Chamberlain tendered his resignation, and by 6pm Churchill was Prime Minister. A few days later, as British forces were being driven back towards the French coast, he walked down the stairs to the War Rooms and headed for the Cabinet Room. Brigadier Leslie Hollis recalled the scene many years later:

> As he looked around the empty room, the poignancy of the moment touched him. No one could say what the news would be within the hour, whether or not England was even then under her first invasion in a thousand years. The little group stood for a moment in silence under the humming fans, each thinking his own thoughts, and then Mr Churchill took his cigar out of his mouth and pointed at the homely wooden chair at the head of the table. 'This is the room from which I'll direct the war,' he said slowly.

Churchill had come to his War Rooms.

Winston Churchill seated at his desk in the No 10 Annexe Map Room, May 1945

THE
ENTRANCE

The door and stairway that are used to enter Churchill War Rooms today did not exist in wartime. Instead staff entered via the government building above (now the Treasury Building, but then known as the New Public Offices).

To enter the War Rooms, staff would first use this entrance to the New Public Offices on Horse Guards Road opposite St James's Park.

Once inside the building, War Rooms personnel would climb another couple of steps before reaching an internal door, shown to the far left of this photo.

Behind this first internal door was Staircase 15, which wound down to the basement level. Having climbed up a number of steps from the street, staff would often take longer than they expected to descend to the basement. This appears to have convinced many that the War Rooms were as much as 50 feet below ground. They were in fact only one floor below ground.

Staircase 15 brought staff into the War Rooms near to where the kitchen is situated in the Churchill Suite. This door was guarded by Royal Marines, which added to a commonly reported impression that going to work in the War Rooms felt like climbing down into the bowels of a ship.

The rather larger door in the centre of this image is the entrance to the No 10 Annexe flat – where Churchill and his family lived from December 1940 onwards – which was immediately above the War Rooms.

Ilene Hutchinson

▶ Gaining access to the War Rooms meant running past a strict set of security checks. Staff were issued with passes like this one (shown front and back), which they were expected to show without fail to the guards as they passed.

'The higher up the officer, the more likely they were to go along with the checking of passes.'

Frank Higgins, military policeman and former guard at the War Rooms

ENTERING THE WAR ROOMS

Shorthand typist Ilene Hutchinson remembers what it was like to make your way into the War Rooms.

'Security was very tough actually. Entering the building... we had to sign on at the times we were scheduled to sign on, and then just fly down the spiral staircase. We had a Marine just on the left of us as we were going down. He was like a waxwork in Madame Tussaud's, just standing there with his rifle at the ready and his red banded hat and not fluttering an eyebrow. Along a passage after the set of stairs, and down some more stairs and then along to the office... We opened the door quietly because there may have been a flap on... You couldn't burst in like you would in an ordinary office.'

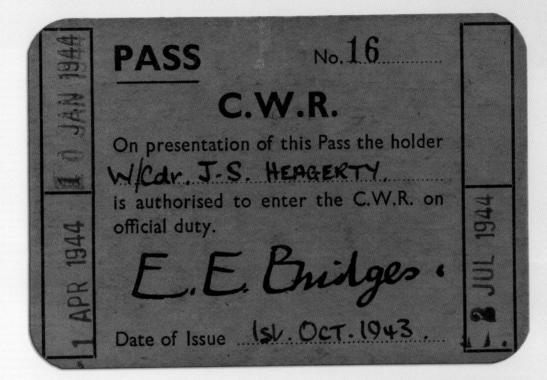

PASS

No. 16

C.W.R.

On presentation of this Pass the holder

W/Cdr. J.S. HEAGERTY.

is authorised to enter the C.W.R. on official duty.

E. E. Bridges.

Date of Issue ....1st. Oct. 1943.

1 0 JAN 1944

1 APR 1944

2 JUL 1944

This Pass is not transferable. If found, it should be handed in at any Police Station, or sent to—

The Camp Commandant,
2, Storey's Gate Building,
S.W.I.

It must be returned when the holder ceases to have duty in the C.W.R.

Signature of Holder *John J. Heagerty*

(S.7518)

THE MAIN CORRIDOR

The main corridor in the War Rooms stretches about 75 metres from one end of the basement to the other, running parallel to Horse Guards Road outside. There were many other corridors to navigate in wartime, but this was the one most frequented by Churchill himself — connecting, as it did, the Cabinet Room, his bedroom, the Map Room, the Transatlantic Telephone Room and many other offices and facilities. Along its walls today there remain many clues to the way that life was conducted underground during the war.

The white metal duct running along the corridor and branching off into every room carried air around the War Rooms. It appears to have served some areas of the basement better than others, with some workers complaining that they suffered from violent headaches because the atmosphere became so foul towards the end of the working day.

The corridors did not merely serve to connect the various sections of the War Rooms together. They also doubled as workplaces when space became especially tight. During the Blitz, for example, typists could be found stationed in some of the alcoves.

The storage chests along the walls of the corridor were used to hold maps that might be required in the Map Room – or more likely by the Joint Planners engaged in devising military strategy for even the most remote theatres of the war.

The main corridor photographed c.1945

'The building to me had masses and masses and masses of corridors. How the heck you ever found your way around I shall never know.'

Leading Aircraftwoman Myra Murden

Wendy Wallace

▲ Fire – either accidental or as a result of a bomb blast – was a major concern in the confines of the War Rooms. Lengths of hose were distributed around the site so that they could be coupled to the main hose, which was positioned next to the fire main outside Room 62A. Other fire-fighting equipment was positioned along the corridor, including buckets of sand like this one. There were also chemical extinguishers, buckets of water and stirrup pumps, as well as axes, shovels and crowbars to deal with possible debris.

◀ The beams, girders and buttresses along the corridor betray the fear of bomb attack. Beams and girders were in place to support the ceiling, and the buttresses were designed to limit damage done by blast waves. Some of the beams can be seen to the left of this photograph.

WORKING IN THE CORRIDORS

Private Secretary Wendy Wallace recalls how the corridors in the War Rooms became part of the site's office space.

'We used to work in the corridors and [Churchill] used to come along and look over one's shoulder to see what you were doing. I was absolutely in awe of him but you got used to having all the notes – the actions of the day – we used to get communications from him all the time... I used to type his speeches before he made them!'

WAY OUT

↓ To G^T· GEORGE

THERE IS TO BE NO WHISTLING OR UNNECESSARY NOISE IN THIS PASSAGE

▲ This sign gives some indication of the serious work undertaken in the War Rooms, but such rules and regulations were not always observed. One veteran, for example, recalls how Map Room officers celebrated Christmas 1941 by racing toilet rolls along the corridor.

◄ The main entrance to the War Rooms was via Horse Guards Road opposite St James's Park, but the building could also be entered from Great George Street. There were several other emergency exits, some of which involved the use of ceiling hatches and ladders.

GENERAL ISMAY

Apart from Churchill himself, Major-General Sir Hastings Ismay was arguably the most important figure in the story of the War Rooms. Before the war, as Secretary to the Committee of Imperial Defence, it was Ismay who made sure that the underground bunker was ready for action. During the war, as Deputy Secretary (Military) to the War Cabinet and Chief of Staff to Churchill, he was the glue that held the War Rooms together, smoothing over the many tensions that arose between the Prime Minister and his military chiefs. After the war, it was Ismay again who helped ensure that the most important rooms in the basement were preserved for posterity.

In September 1939, Room 61 was partitioned to create Room 61 Right for Ismay and Room 61 Left for his two Private Secretaries. Both rooms were taken over by the Joint Planning Staff in the summer of 1940, but reverted to their original occupants from early 1943 onwards, when they proved especially useful during the V-weapon offensives of 1944 and 1945. The telephone shown here, with its stark cautionary message, is displayed on the desk in Room 61 Left.

Although Ismay only made sporadic use of this room, he was a frequent visitor to the War Rooms – finding the draw of the Map Room especially hard to resist. He later wrote that 'when a big battle or critical movement was in progress, it was a temptation to find pretexts for going to the [Map Room] at all hours of the day and night'. He likened the experience to visiting a friend in hospital: 'One entered the room hoping for the best, but fearing the worst.'

At the touch of one of these buttons, Ismay could summon his junior officers from their room next door, or connect to the Prime Minister's quarters and the War Cabinet Room.

The addition of carpet to Ismay's room is the most obvious indication that it was used by a senior officer. There are also other differences, such as the desk and the lamp, and the extra-wide bed.

Detail of a document box on display in the room manned by Ismay's Private Secretaries. One of his staff's duties was to establish the administrative arrangements for the Prime Minister's foreign conferences and trips.

▲ A surviving copy of the government's 'C.W.R Standing Instructions' for the War Rooms includes an instruction for heaters like this one to be turned off whenever a room was left empty – an example of wartime economy, even here at the centre of power.

▶ Two officers manned this room to assist Ismay. One was Commander Maurice 'Senior' Knott; the other was Lieutenant Ian McEwan, who was inevitably known as 'Junior'.

Wooden props and beams such as those in this room can be seen throughout the War Rooms. They were installed before the war as a crude precaution against the possible collapse of the building above during an air raid.

SIR EDWARD BRIDGES

As Secretary to the War Cabinet, Sir Edward Bridges was the most senior civil servant in the land. It was his job to call meetings of the War Cabinet, organise the agenda, prepare and circulate minutes and make sure that all of the decisions taken were implemented. Together with Ismay, to whom he delegated all military matters arising from the War Cabinet, Bridges was key to Britain's war effort. The pair were described by Churchill's Private Secretary Sir John Colville as 'the twin pillars on which the Prime Minister rested'.

In autumn 1939, the room allocated to Bridges was partitioned so that it could also accommodate his personal secretary, Sir Ronald Harris, and one or more assistant secretaries.

◄ The right-hand room used by Sir Edward Bridges himself is afforded the luxury of a small carpet, but is otherwise extremely basic. Described by Churchill as 'a man of exceptional force, ability and personal charm', Bridges is said to have adopted an unobtrusive leadership style built on tact, diplomacy and cooperation.

▼ Writing equipment displayed in Bridges' room. Charged with keeping Britain's war machine running smoothly, he is said to have actively favoured using this underground room, especially during the Blitz. Bridges was present at practically every one of the 1,188 War Cabinet meetings held during the war, and was party to information of the utmost secrecy.

'Sir Edward Bridges, son of a poet, with a poet's unruly hair, a man of shy charm, held his high post with such modesty that he managed to merge his considerable intellect into a balanced whole of unobtrusive leadership and tactful cooperation with colleagues trimmed for war.'

Description of Sir Edward Bridges by Joan Bright Astley, a senior War Rooms secretary

When Bridges' room was partitioned in 1939, the left-hand side was allocated to three of his assistant secretaries, while Bridges shared the right-hand room with his personal secretary Sir Ronald Harris. This arrangement was soon changed so that Harris and one assistant secretary used this left-hand room, leaving Bridges with quarters to himself.

SIR JOHN MARTIN

In 1944 and 1945 Room 66B was occupied by Sir John Martin, Churchill's Principal Private Secretary. It was Martin's role to run the Prime Minister's office, managing his diary, accompanying him to meetings at home and abroad, and dealing with all his incoming and outgoing correspondence. At his desk in this room, he would also act as Churchill's gatekeeper, ensuring that no-one gained undue access to the Prime Minister.

◀ Martin would have made most use of this room during the V-weapon offensive, which saw V1 flying bombs and later V2 rockets target London.

▼ Mounted above the door to the office, this sign was a reminder for visitors that they were nearing the Prime Minister's own quarters, which lie just five or six metres along a private corridor.

THE
CABINET ROOM

The existence of the entire War Rooms complex was born out of the need to create a safe meeting room where the War Cabinet could convene during enemy bombing raids. Here the Prime Minister, his key ministers and advisers would meet with the Chiefs of Staff to make decisions of extraordinary significance. Here too the Chiefs of Staff would hold their own discussions, and Churchill would chair meetings of the Defence Committee, which he set up on becoming Prime Minister. It is a room which has hardly changed in the decades since, and the details it contains cast a great deal of insight into what it must have been like to attend one of the many fateful meetings held within its spartan confines.

The entrance to the Cabinet Room consists of two doors, both of which were locked and guarded when a meeting was in progress. One sentry stood outside the outer door, the other was posted in the tiny lobby dividing the room from the corridor.

The inner of the two doors leading into the
Cabinet Room was fitted with a glass-covered slit.
This allowed the sentry to see what was going on
inside the room but without being able to hear a
word of what was said. Secrecy was paramount.

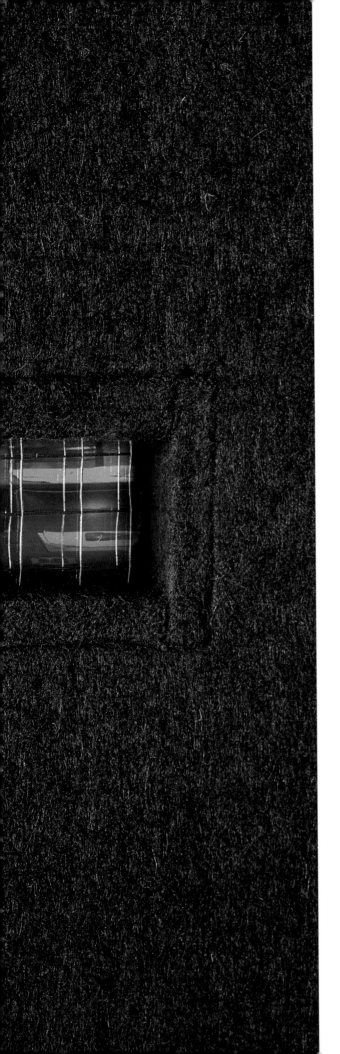

General Sir Hastings Ismay, August 1945

THE WAR CABINET SYSTEM

During the war, General Ismay was asked to write a summary of how the War Cabinet system worked. He had this to say about its meetings:

'The War Cabinet meets every day, sometimes twice a day. The morning meeting invariably starts with reports by the Services on the military situation, and by the Foreign Secretary on political developments. Thereafter the War Cabinet addresses itself to whatever problems may have been put before it, in the shape of strategical reports by the Chiefs of Staff, or memoranda on any and every problem which requires to be resolved, from the Ministers, Committees or Departments concerned.'

The room has been preserved to look the way it would have done moments before a meeting of the War Cabinet held there at 5pm on 15 October 1940. Bombs had caused severe damage to 10 Downing Street the previous evening, and this had finally persuaded Churchill to meet in the War Rooms on a regular basis.

One of the most remarkable features of the room is the way in which the tables have been laid out to create a central well with enough space for three seats. It was in this crucible that the heads of the Army, Navy and Air Force would sit — eyeball to eyeball with the Prime Minister, who would be hunched in the rounded wooden chair opposite. Given Churchill's propensity to push his military chiefs as far beyond their comfort zones as they could bear, it was an arrangement frought with tension and confrontation.

In peacetime any minutes and conclusions arising from a Cabinet meeting were the sole responsibility of the Secretary to the Cabinet. In wartime a succession of Assistant Secretaries would attend different sections of the meetings, and then leave the room to get on with the minuting process. This meant that the minutes and conclusions of a morning meeting of the War Cabinet could be circulated by 3 or 4pm the same day.

The words displayed on the conference table were spoken by Queen Victoria when she was presented with a gloomy report on progress in the Boer War: 'Please understand there is no depression in this house and we are not interested in the possibilities of defeat, they do not exist.' A copy was presented to President George W Bush during his visit to the War Rooms in 2001.

The Cabinet Room photographed c.1945

▲ The wooden arms of Churchill's chair are gouged with scratch marks that speak volumes for the nervous energy of its occupant and the tension of the hundreds of meetings that he presided over in this room. The marks differ on each arm. Churchill's right hand appears to have scratched at the wood, while the signet ring on his left made deeper gouges.

◀ The same maps hang on the walls now as during the war. Churchill himself sat in front of a map of the world, but it is unlikely that it served any practical purpose during a meeting.

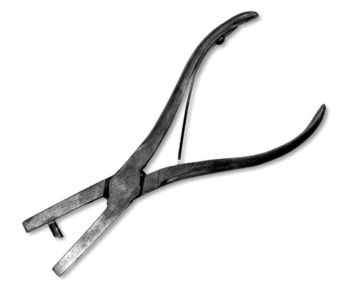

▲ Churchill used to insist that all documents in the War Rooms were punched and tagged rather than stapled or paper-clipped. The device sitting in front of him on the table was his preferred type of hole punch, which he used to refer to as a 'klop'. He didn't always get his way. One member of staff remembers stapling a document and sending it to the Prime Minister, who promptly cut his finger on it.

▶ Like all British government ministers, Churchill used a specially made red box to carry his State papers with him wherever he went. The position of the handle and lock ensured that the box had to be locked before it could be picked up. The Barbados sticker was added by Churchill's son Randolph.

During meetings in the War Cabinet Room, Churchill is reported to have thrown his cigar butts over his shoulder and into a fire bucket. The story goes that the marine orderlies would collect them up after a meeting and sell them.

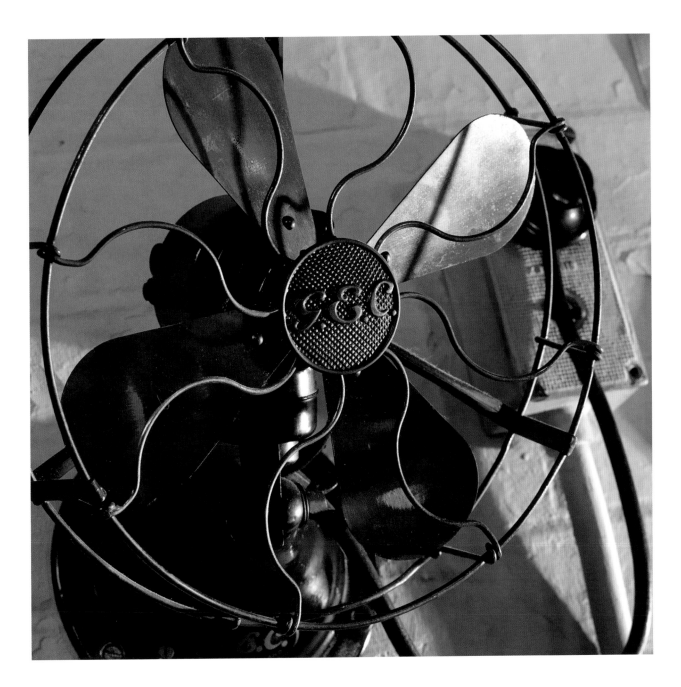

The white metal ventilation duct, which snakes around the ceiling of the room, was installed in the autumn of 1939. It was the last improvement required to make the room fit for purpose. Small electric fans were also mounted on the walls to improve the atmosphere in the room, but they could do little more than keep circulating the clouds of cigarette and cigar smoke billowing up from the table.

2

THE DARKEST DAYS

May 1940 to May 1941

Three days after Winston Churchill became Prime Minister, he stood up to address Parliament: 'We have before us many, many long months of struggle and of suffering,' he said. He was right. Hitler's troops were already pushing the British Army back to the Channel, and the French Army was on the verge of disintegration. By 27 May the men of the British Expeditionary Force would be clambering onto boats at Dunkirk and heading back to Britain – a Britain that was about to come under siege.

Continuing his speech Churchill declared: 'You ask, what is our policy? I can say: It is to wage war, by sea, land and air, with all our might and with all the strength that God can give us… You ask, what is our aim? I can answer in one word: It is victory, victory at all costs, victory in spite of all terror, victory, however long and hard the road may be; for without victory, there is no survival.'

They were brave words and well received, but the truth was that the policies and aims of the government were not so set in stone. From 26 to 28 May, as the evacuation from Dunkirk was getting under way, Churchill was locked in tense discussions with his five-man War Cabinet. The agenda was profoundly simple: should Britain fight on or should the government negotiate a peace? Churchill was for fighting,

but he faced being out-voted by his colleagues. It was only by gathering support among the more junior members of the government that he carried the day.

By 4 June, the operation at Dunkirk was complete. Against all the odds, over 337,000 British and allied troops had escaped capture – far more than Churchill had dared hope. 'The successful evacuation of the BEF has revolutionised the Home Defence position,' he wrote to Ismay, his spirits lifted by the lifeline, however short-lived, that the evacuation had provided. Anticipating a German invasion he dismissed all talk of a negotiated peace once and for all, telling Parliament: 'We shall fight on the beaches, we shall fight on the landing grounds, we shall fight in the fields and in the streets, we shall fight in the hills; we shall never surrender.'

Churchill projected an infectious sense of confidence, but he was by no means sure of victory. Ten days after this iconic speech, he turned to Ismay and said: 'Do you realise we probably have a maximum of three months to live?' It was a remark made in good humour but it gives some indication of the private burden that he was carrying. He also became so uncharacteristically brusque with staff at the War Rooms and 10 Downing Street that, on 23 June, his wife Clementine was moved to write him a letter, warning him 'that there is a danger of your being generally disliked by your colleagues and subordinates because of your rough sarcastic and overbearing manner'. Fearing how her words would be received, she promptly tore the letter up but then decided to send it to him after all.

Churchill wasn't the only one feeling the pressure. Following the fall of France, staff at the War Rooms were struggling to adjust to new priorities. In the months since the start of the war, the layout and function of the underground facility had become relatively well established – although not without a good deal of change and experimentation. Two chief purposes had emerged: to gather intelligence on the war, and to provide an emergency meeting place for the War Cabinet and the Chiefs of Staff.

The heart of the underground complex throughout the war – and at any hour of day or night – was the Map Room. It was here that information on every development in every theatre of the war was gathered, collated and presented on the maps adorning its walls. It was from here too that a daily summary of the war was distributed every morning to the Prime Minister, the Chiefs of Staff and the King, and an intelligence briefing given to the Chiefs of Staff before they went into conference.

Given the importance of the Map Room, the Chiefs of Staff found it convenient to carry out most of their conferences in the underground rooms. This in turn made it useful for their administrative staff to work on site, and for the Joint Planners to stay in close attendance. By the time Churchill became Prime Minister a suite of 15 rooms was in use, providing working and living accommodation for some 60 people. It was a bigger facility than had originally been planned, but it would prove to be nowhere near big enough.

After the fall of France, the risk of a German invasion made it imperative to establish an Advanced Headquarters for Britain's Home Forces at the War Rooms. That way, the Prime Minister and Chiefs of Staff could have direct access to the Commander-in-Chief of the Home Forces. A hasty reorganisation saw this Advanced Headquarters housed in Rooms 62, 62A and 62B. The Map Room Annexe was handed over to Home Forces intelligence officers and a quarter of the Map Room – the holiest of holies – was also set aside for their use.

Alan Brooke, the newly appointed Commander-in-Chief of the Home Forces, visited his underground office on 29 July. After the war he described the set-up as excellent but, mindful of Churchill's capacity for interference, he identified one fault: 'its proximity to Winston!' This was demonstrated from day one, with Brooke's diary recording that he was invited by the Prime Minister to attend part of the War Cabinet meeting – the first to be held in the War Rooms since Churchill had taken office. Brooke described the experience as 'interesting', but the two men would go on to have many clashes around the same table.

By the time of Brooke's appointment Churchill had made several changes to the way in which the war was run. He had pared his War Cabinet down to five men, with the service ministers and Chiefs of Staff attending as required. This was now the forum for discussing any problem, military or civil, on which a decision could only be reached at the highest level. There were other changes too. Churchill combined the office of Prime Minister with the Minister of Defence and established various committees through which he could enjoy direct contact with his Chiefs of Staff. As a result he could now exercise direct supervision not only over military policy and planning, but also the day-to-day conduct of operations.

Yet powerful as he was, Churchill was no dictator. Sir Ian Jacob, the Military Assistant Secretary to the War Cabinet, recalled how the Prime Minister 'pushed and pushed and pushed, which was all to the good provided he had people to keep him on the rails'. If he disagreed with the advice of his Chiefs of Staff, he would argue his case strenuously, but if they held their ground, he would almost always give them his backing. It was this combination of push and pull, according to Jacob, that helped to win the war.

Shortly after becoming Prime Minister, Churchill was given his own bedroom study in the War Rooms, right next door to the Map Room. The expectation that he might soon have need of such a refuge was easily understandable. Throughout August 1940, RAF fighter squadrons were engaging Luftwaffe bombers and fighters in the skies over southern England. Dubbed the Battle of Britain, it was seen as the prelude to the German invasion, which was expected at almost any moment. Until 7 September the chief targets attacked by the Germans were

Winston Churchill visits bombed-out buildings in the East End of London on 8 September 1940

the RAF's forward air bases and coastal defences, but they then switched attention to bombing London itself.

This was the Blitz – the sustained aerial bombardment that Britain's political and military leaders had long expected. It was fear of such a bombardment that had led to the preparation of the War Rooms, and the full capabilities of the facility would be put to the most severe of tests over the course of the next nine months. In September it played host to most evening meetings of the

War Cabinet, and in October and November almost every top-level meeting was held there – whether of the War Cabinet, the Defence Committee or the Chiefs of Staff.

On 11 September, just days after the beginning of the Blitz, the Prime Minister made use of the War Rooms' broadcasting facilities for the first time. Sitting at his bedroom desk, he gave one of his most stirring orations – condemning the bombing raids on London and the south-east, giving a stark warning about the possibility of invasion, and issuing a rallying cry for every man and woman to do their duty.

The bombing raids were becoming uncomfortably close. The Ministry of Transport, just a short walk away from the War Rooms, was damaged on 12 September, and Buckingham Palace, just on the other side of St James's Park, was dive-bombed the following evening. In fact, news of this attack was handed to the Prime Minister in the War Rooms, while he was presiding over an evening meeting of the War Cabinet.

On 16 September, as the raids continued, Churchill was persuaded to stay the night in his subterranean bedroom for the first time. He did not enjoy the experience. In fact he loathed the idea of seeking out shelter during an attack, preferring if possible to stay above ground or, better still, to find a rooftop from which to view proceedings. By the end of the war, he is thought to have spent only a handful of nights in his War Rooms bed.

During the first few days of the Blitz, however, Churchill and his staff found themselves underground rather more than they would have liked. Churchill's private secretary, John Colville, noted in his diary that 'much of the time, both by day and by night, is being spent in the disagreeable atmosphere of the Central War Room'. Churchill too seemed resigned to the prospect, writing to Neville Chamberlain on 21 September that he proposed 'to lead a troglodyte existence'.

In truth, Churchill lived the life of a nomad, working and staying the night in a variety of locations – 10 Downing Street, Parliament, his country home of Chequers and the War Rooms. On several evenings he also made use of the London Underground offices situated at the disused Down Street station, complete with hot running water, fully plumbed toilet system and well-stocked wine cellar.

For the rest of the War Rooms staff, a night spent underground was somewhat less comfortable. Beneath the War Rooms lies another floor that stretches the full length and breadth of the building above. Its ceiling was uncomfortably low and you had to stoop to get through its doorways, many of which were no more than four feet high. It was known unaffectionately as 'the dock'.

Every night dozens of staff, wrapped modestly in their all-enveloping dressing gowns, would duck their way down the steps, carrying their sheets to any free bed they could find in the spartan dormitories below. Despite the exhaustion brought on by their long working hours, sleep did not always come easily. Some were disturbed by the rattle and hum of the air conditioning system, which seemed to have little effect on the heat or the fug of cigarette smoke. Others were kept awake by the scamperings of rats and bugs, or by the foul smell of the chemical toilets positioned behind crudely constructed screens. It is little wonder that many sought out quiet spots to sleep in the floors above – despite the danger and noise of the Luftwaffe's bombs. Others even preferred to risk the journey home instead.

The increased reliance on the War Rooms as a refuge made it all the more alarming when Churchill discovered late in September 1940 that the site itself was not, as he had assumed, bomb-proof. He immediately ordered the construction of a thick concrete slab above the ceiling, and the addition of an exterior apron wall at ground-floor level. He also insisted that a valuable section of the underground space near the Map Room Annexe be filled in with cement because it was located beneath a staircase and was therefore more vulnerable to attack. Churchill's interest in this slab did not end with the issue of the order for its construction. His was a much more hands-on role, as his private secretary John Colville recalls:

> I remember two or three times having to go with him in the evenings with torches down to where they were putting up traverses and other brickwork in the basement in order to make the building stronger. And he used to go along and comment on them. There was one great occasion when he climbed up on one of the traverses...jumped down the other side...and landed in a pool of liquid cement, which I thought rather funny! I looked over the wall at him and I said: 'I think, sir, that you have met your Waterloo.'

However inconvenient and noisy it was to have workmen crawling all over the site, everyone could see the necessity for the work. In fact, matters became more urgent following a raid on 14 October when shockwaves from nearby blasts caused damage to the Prime Minister's residence at 10 Downing Street. It was this incident that persuaded Churchill to hold meetings in the War Rooms on a more regular basis, beginning with the War Cabinet meeting at 5pm on 15 October. This is the moment in time captured on all the clocks in Churchill War Rooms today.

The same incident also prompted confirmation of a plan to move the Prime Minister's offices and living quarters to the building above the War Rooms (now the Treasury Building). These quarters, which would become known as the No 10 Annexe, were relatively strongly built and gave Churchill direct access to the War Rooms beneath. The move also helped the Prime Minister's staff pin him down in one main location rather than try to predict where he might choose to work, eat and sleep from one day to the next. His movements had become so difficult to track that several of his staff were taken in by a mock minute prepared by his private secretary John Peck at the end of October:

Action This Day

Pray let six new offices be fitted for my use, in Selfridge's, Lambeth Palace, Stanmore, Tooting Bec, the Palladium and Mile End Road. I will inform you at 6 each evening at which office I shall dine work and sleep. Accommodation will be required for Mrs Churchill, two shorthand-typists, three secretaries and Nelson [the No.10 cat]. There should be a shelter for all and a place for me to watch air-raids from the roof. This should be completed by Monday. There is to be no hammering during office hours, that is between 7am and 3am.

WSC

The Churchills moved into the No 10 Annexe in December 1940. The onset of winter – and the losses sustained by the Luftwaffe during the Battle of Britain – meant that the prospect of an invasion now seemed much less likely. Nonetheless, the chances of a British victory remained remote, and the spring of 1941 brought no relief. Bombs continued to rain down over London night after night, while workmen below the Annexe extended the concrete slab to bring steadily more rooms under its protection. By the beginning of May 1941, a further 34 rooms had been made available. This meant that a telephone exchange, first-aid room and canteen could be added, as well as a suite of rooms for the emergency use of the Prime Minister and his wife, personal staff and key ministers.

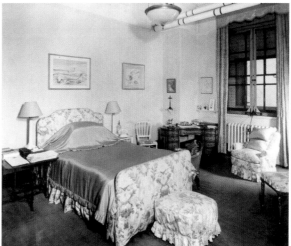

Top From December 1940 onwards the Prime Minister and his wife lived mainly in the No 10 Annexe flat, adapted from ground floor offices directly above the Cabinet War Rooms. Mrs Churchill decorated the flat in attractive colours and with their own pictures and furniture, but when possible they entertained in 10 Downing Street.
Bottom Clementine Churchill's bedroom in the No 10 Annexe.

As it turned out, London suffered the last heavy raid of the Blitz on 10 May, so the rooms in the 'Churchill Suite' were rarely used. After nine long months of bombing, Hitler was ready to launch an invasion – but it would not be an assault on Britain. Instead he was about to turn his attention to the Soviet Union, in what would prove to be one of the most pivotal decisions in the war.

THE DOCK

Despite its low ceilings and poor ventilation, the sub-basement below the War Rooms – known as the 'dock' – was also put to use during the war, when pressure for room in the main basement level became more acute.

Museum records reveal that all sorts of items were found in the sub-basement when IWM began work on restoring the floor above. There were sinks, fire buckets, stepladders, stretchers, ink bottles, mail bags, in-trays and much more – reflecting the wider use to which the dock was put during the war. Many of the objects were used in the restoration of the War Rooms, but many others are now held in storage.

Most of the doorways in the dock were extremely low, forcing staff to stoop to get through. The addition of ventilation trunking in the sub-basement further reduced the ceiling height in many of the rooms, and added a constant low-level noise to the list of irritants for staff.

TO ROOMS

60, 60ᴬ 61, 61ᴬ 62, 62ᴬ
64,   65

Elizabeth Layton

▲ According to the Standing Instructions for March 1943 there were 22 of these chemical toilets in the sub-basement – 13 set aside for men, 9 for women. Anyone who wanted to use plumbed-in toilets had to head up two floors, watched all the way by the ever-present Royal Marine guards.

◀ For the most part the dock was reserved for overnight accommodation, which meant it saw intensive use during the Blitz of 1940–1941 and the V-weapon offensive of 1944–1945. But some unfortunate staff had to make the trip down the stairs every day – not to grab some sleep, but to work in the most dismal of offices.

SLEEPING IN THE DOCK

One of Churchill's secretaries, Elizabeth Layton, describes what it was like to sleep down in the dock:

'When sleeping in the shelter after late duty, one would retire to the bathroom in the floor above to put on one's night attire (taken from the suitcase out of which one lived) and hurry down several flights of stairs, past the War Rooms to the bedroom level below. By this time one was safely past meeting anyone. But when, having slept heavily for six hours, to the roar of the air-conditioning, in a narrow cot covered with army blankets, one would emerge from one's room, there were all sorts of people whom one wished to avoid. As one hurried up the stairs, heavy-eyed, in one's dressing gown, one always seemed to meet the sprucest, haughtiest, most glamorous officers coming the other way.'

Sleeping quarters and emergency kitchen photographed c.1945

Although the War Rooms staff were grateful to have accommodation provided, few of them found it easy to sleep in the uncomfortable surroundings of the dock. The air conditioning rattled and hummed, and did little to improve the smoky, hot and humid atmosphere. The smell of chemical toilets wafted up and down the corridors, while rats and bugs were often seen scuttling across floors and beds.

THE
BROADCASTING
ROOM

The decision to install broadcasting equipment was taken very early on in the planning of the War Rooms. After the war the room was stripped, but its contents have since been carefully restored. Mr H J Gregory, one of the BBC engineers who worked here during the war, acted as an adviser on the project.

The machinery in Room 60 Left made it possible for Churchill to make four major speeches from his bedroom study. The first was on 11 September 1940, exhorting Britons to prepare for a German invasion. The second was a broadcast to the French Empire on 21 October 1940, and the third to the people of Italy two months later. The last came on 8 December 1941 in response to the Japanese attack on the US fleet at Pearl Harbor.

The equipment on display in the Broadcasting Room could still be used to make a transmission. It was sourced from the BBC's own stores, and retired BBC engineer John Ireland volunteered to set it all up in 1983.

BBC technicians arranged for microphones to be set up in the Prime Minister's bedroom study and in the Cabinet Room. The latter involved suspending the microphone from an ingenious counter-balanced contraption above the Prime Minister's chair – a sketch of which can be found in the museum's files.

◀ Churchill's wife Clementine also made use of the broadcasting facilities to make radio appeals in support of the Aid to Russia campaign, through which Britain helped to keep the Soviet Union in the war.

▼ According to Mr H J Gregory, who assisted with broadcasts from the Cabinet War Rooms during the war, Churchill would usually call for a broadcast at very short notice. The team would only find out at the last minute whether it was to be made from the War Rooms, 10 Downing Street or Chequers. Luckily it took no time at all to prepare the equipment.

'No one should blind himself to the fact that a heavy full-scale invasion of this island is being prepared with all the usual German thoroughness and method and that it may be launched at any time now upon England, upon Scotland, or upon Ireland, or upon all three. If this invasion is going to be tried at all, it does not seem that it can be long delayed... Therefore, we must regard the next week or so as a very important week for us in our history. It ranks with the days when the Spanish Armada was approaching the Channel and Drake was finishing his game of bowls, or when Nelson stood between us and Napoleon's Grand Army at Boulogne. We have read about all this in the history books, but what is happening now is on a far greater scale and of far more consequence to the life and future of the world and its civilisation than those brave old days of the past. Every man and woman will therefore prepare himself and herself to do his duty whatever it may be, with special pride and care.'

Extract from a speech broadcast by Churchill from the War Rooms on 11 September 1940

GHQ,
HOME FORCES

In spring 1940 a General Headquarters for Britain's Home Forces was set up at St Paul's School in Hammersmith, a couple of miles away from the War Rooms. Its staff would be responsible for coordinating the defence of Britain in the unlikely event – or so it seemed at the time – of a German invasion. After the fall of France, the threat of invasion became all too real, and arrangements were made to establish an Advanced Headquarters for the Home Forces in the War Rooms. That way the Prime Minister and Chiefs of Staff would be able to communicate directly with the Commander-in-Chief of the Home Forces. Hasty preparations were therefore made to free up Rooms 62, 62A and 62B for this purpose.

Six senior Home Forces officers worked in Room 62A, displacing several members of the Joint Planning Staff who had used the room for a few months at the beginning of 1940.

◀ Room 62A later became a Mess Room for the Royal Marines.

▼ Room 62 was fitted out as an office for junior members of the Home Forces staff. Four other rooms were also made available in the sub-basement – a signals room for seven members of staff, a cipher room, and two offices housing 15 clerks between them. Little is known about how these rooms were actually laid out during their occupation by the Home Forces, but CWR historians do know that five junior officers were expected to work in this space.

◀ To cope with any attempted invasion, the officers stationed in this Advanced Headquarters needed to be in constant contact with the General Headquarters for the Home Forces in Hammersmith — and with all their individual Home Forces units. To help make this possible, a tent was erected in St James's Park to accommodate ten signal despatch riders.

▼ Stirrup pumps like this one were designed to help deal with any outbreaks of fire. It took two or three people to operate — one to direct the nozzle, a second to pump the water from a bucket (kept full at all times), and ideally a third to replenish the bucket.

General Sir Alan Brooke, c.1941

GENERAL SIR ALAN BROOKE

As Commander-in-Chief of Britain's Home Forces, General Sir Alan Brooke was responsible for defending the country against German invasion. In this diary entry from 15 September 1940 he describes the burden he carried:

'Still no move on the part of the Germans! Everything remains keyed up for an early invasion, and the air war goes on unabated. The coming week must remain a critical one, and it is hard to see how Hitler can now retrace his steps and stop the invasion. The suspense of waiting is very trying, especially when one is familiar with the weakness of our defence! Our exposed coastline is just twice the length of the front the French were holding in France with about 80 divisions and a Maginot Line! Here we have 22 divisions of which only about half can be looked upon as in any way fit for any form of mobile operation! ... A responsibility such as that of the defence of this country under the existing conditions is one that weighs on one like a ton of bricks, and it is hard at times to retain the hopeful, confident exterior which is so essential to retain the confidence of those under one, and to guard against their having any doubts as regards final success.'

Between July 1940 and January 1941 Room 62B acted as the emergency accommodation for General Sir Alan Brooke, at that time the Commander-in-Chief of the Home Forces. It was later assigned to the 'Camp Commandant', the man responsible for the day-to-day maintenance of the War Rooms. This key rack, containing keys to every room in the complex, dates back to that part of the room's occupation.

THE MAP ROOM ANNEXE

Room 64 is one of the few areas in the War Rooms that fulfilled much the same purpose throughout the war. Situated next door to the main Map Room, it was referred to as its Annexe. It became a focal point for the growing number of Joint Planning Staff officers who could not be accommodated in the Map Room, but who nonetheless needed access to its maps.

Today the Map Room Annexe acts more like a corridor than a room, but it is actually arranged in much the same way as it appeared during the war. It also contains several features that give an insight into its original use.

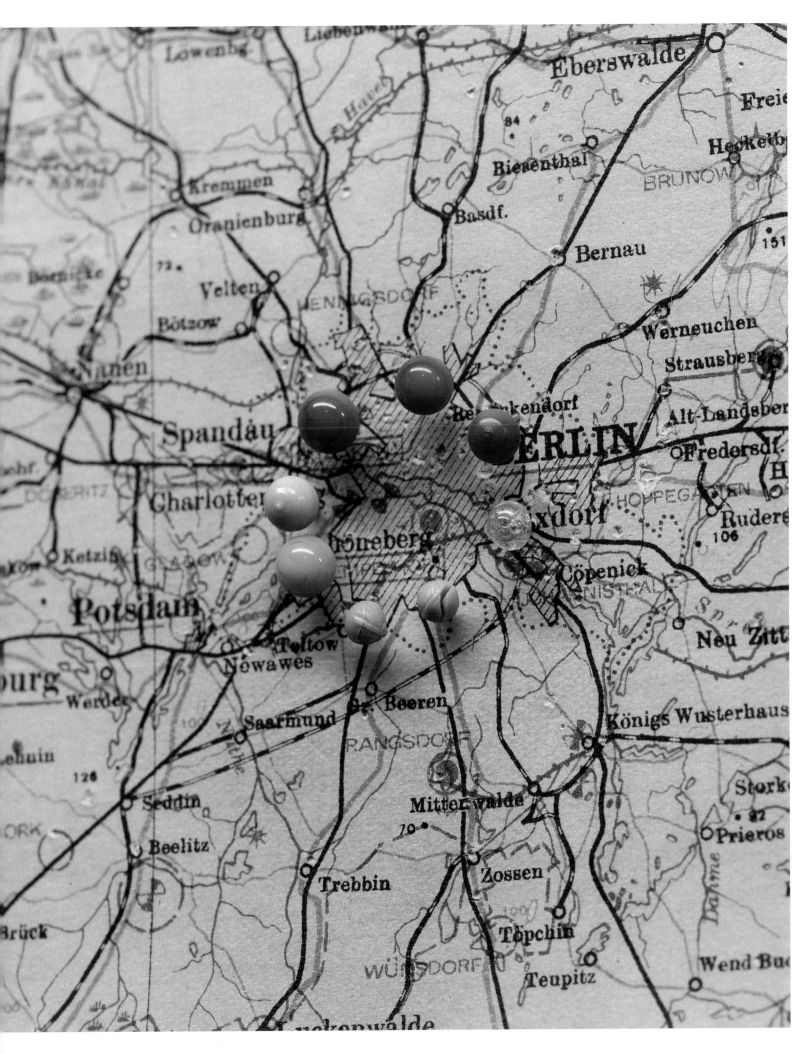

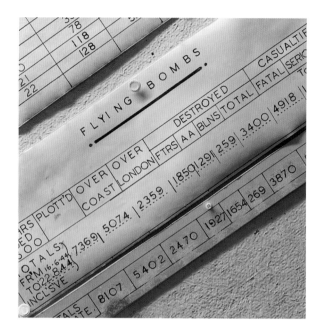

▲ Part of the work of the Joint Planning and Joint Intelligence Staff was to collate, analyse and issue reports on all sorts of aspects of the war. This table was compiled to record the effects of the first two months of V1 'flying bomb' attacks in 1944.

▶ This telephone switch frame allowed officers in the War Rooms to make secure phone calls from their rooms. Only one scrambling device was available for such calls, so this switch frame was installed to allow the officers to share its use.

The large map on one wall of the Annexe spent much of the war hanging in the main Map Room. It charts in great detail the devastating advance of the German forces in Russia in 1941–1942 and their gradual retreat in the years that followed.

◀ The map also shows the boundaries imposed on Eastern Europe in 1945 – a clue to one of the later preoccupations of the Joint Planning Staff as they looked ahead to the uncertainties of the post-war world.

▼ The walls of the Map Room Annexe were lined with boards so that maps and charts could be pinned up, marked and labelled, as and when required.

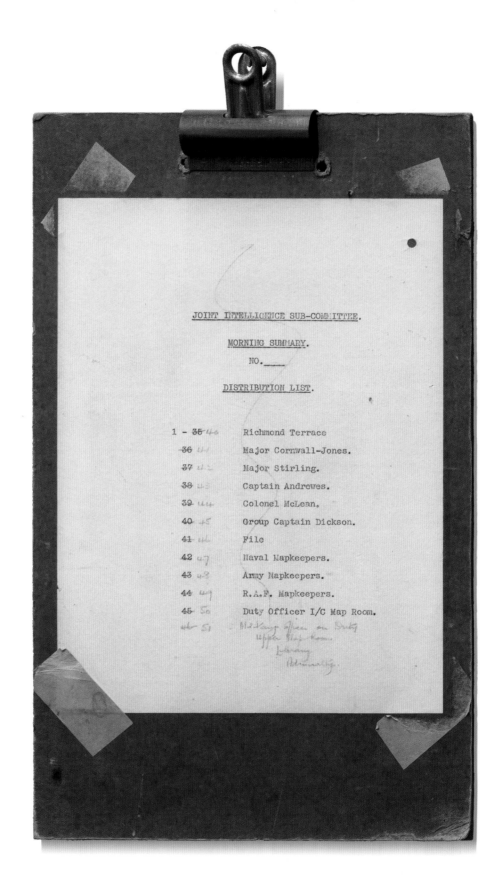

JOINT INTELLIGENCE SUB-COMMITTEE.

MORNING SUMMARY.

NO.____

DISTRIBUTION LIST.

1 - 35 46   Richmond Terrace
36 41   Major Cornwall-Jones.
37 42   Major Stirling.
38 43   Captain Andrewes.
39 44   Colonel McLean.
40 45   Group Captain Dickson.
41 46   File
42 47   Naval Mapkeepers.
43 48   Army Mapkeepers.
44 49   R.A.F. Mapkeepers.
45 50   Duty Officer I/C Map Room.
46 51   Military officer on Duty
            Upper Map Room
            Library
            Admiralty.

COOLING ↓ CONTROL

STARTING SWITCH

START OFF STOP

FAN SPEED

RESET NORMAL LOW

PUSH RESET IF UNIT FAILS TO COOL WHEN THE ROOM
TEMPERATURE IS ABOVE COOLING CONTROL SETTING.

FRIGIDAIRE

MADE IN U.S.A.

▲ The main air conditioning system installed in the War Rooms was never especially efficient, so in some places it was supplemented by the addition of American Frigidaire units. There was one each in the Map Room and the Map Room Annexe, and several more were installed elsewhere in the basement.

◄ Pinned to one of the columns in the Annexe is a distribution list for the morning summary, prepared daily by the Joint Intelligence Staff. Though not directly named on the list, Churchill took a great interest in the work of his intelligence gatherers.

INTERNAL DEFENCES

The War Rooms faced two main threats during the war — the possibility of a bomb strike, and an attack on Whitehall by airborne German troops. At intervals around the site you can see clues to the type of defence precautions that were put in place to protect the command centre.

If the War Rooms came under ground attack, the bulk of its defence would be carried out by a platoon of Grenadier Guards permanently stationed at its main entrance, one floor up in the building above. The entrances at basement level would be manned by the Royal Marine orderlies who undertook a variety of day-to-day duties around the site. Any Map Room or Joint Planning officers were expected to arm themselves from gun racks like this one, muster outside the Map Room or Room 62B and then act as a reserve for the Marines. The Camp Commandant or the Map Room Duty Officer would direct the defence, using the Map Room as a command headquarters.

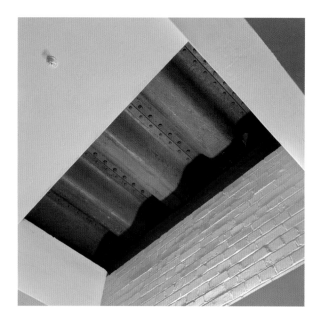

▲ When Churchill discovered in autumn 1940 that the War Rooms were not bomb-proof, he ordered the construction of a concrete slab between the basement ceiling and the ground floor of the building above. A cross-section of part of this slab can be seen in the War Rooms today, complete with its steel waffle containment and support girders.

▶ This section of the War Rooms was filled in with concrete in the winter of 1940 as part of efforts to make the complex more bomb-resistant. When a bomb fell close by later in the war, sending shockwaves through the building, Churchill remarked: 'A pity it was not a bit nearer, so that we might have tested our defences.'

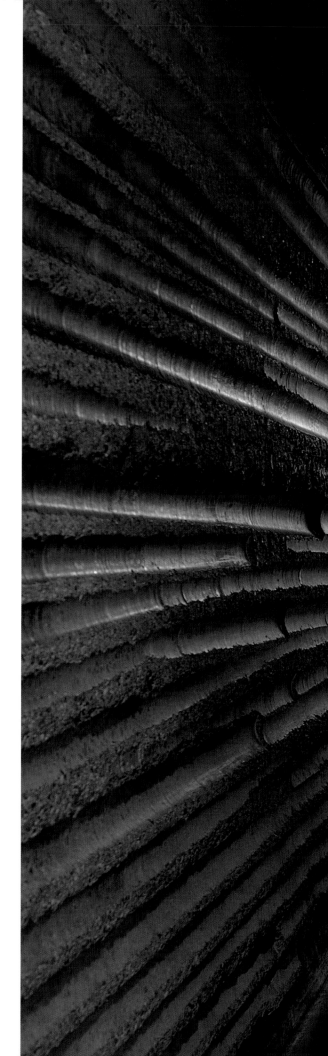

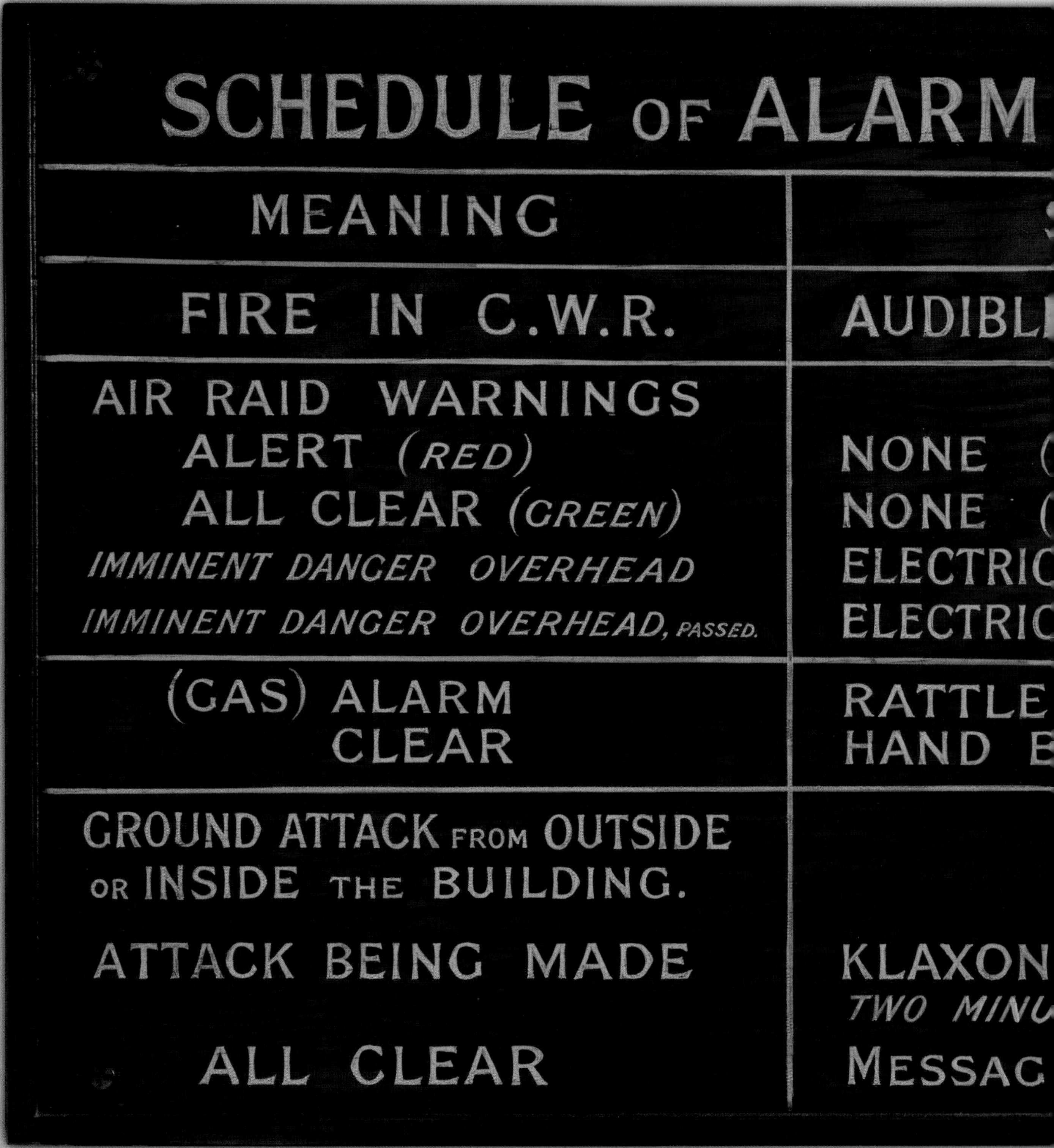

SCHEDULE of ALARM

MEANING	
FIRE IN C.W.R.	AUDIBL
AIR RAID WARNINGS	
ALERT (*RED*)	NONE
ALL CLEAR (*GREEN*)	NONE
IMMINENT DANGER OVERHEAD	ELECTRIC
IMMINENT DANGER OVERHEAD, PASSED.	ELECTRIC
(GAS) ALARM	RATTLE
CLEAR	HAND B
GROUND ATTACK FROM OUTSIDE OR INSIDE THE BUILDING.	
ATTACK BEING MADE	KLAXON
	TWO MINU
ALL CLEAR	MESSAG

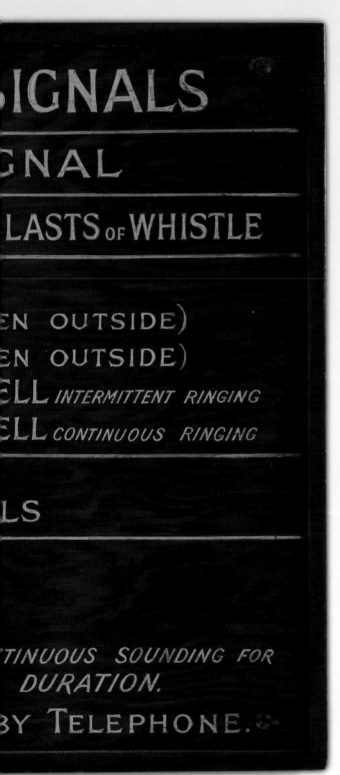

Every member of staff at the War Rooms was expected to make themselves familiar with the Standing Instructions – a set of instructions explaining what to do in case of various emergencies. This 'schedule of alarm signals' was also posted up on one of the walls as a reminder, detailing the meaning of all the whistles, bells, rattles and klaxons that might suddenly begin to sound out.

The alarm signal for a ground attack was a two-minute long blast on a klaxon horn. If it sounded, any women trained to provide First Aid were expected to head to the First Aid room that was added to the site in spring 1941. All telephonists were told to report to the Switchboard room, while all other women were advised to remain at their posts or stay in their rooms. Any unarmed men were told to gather next door to the Cabinet Room and await further instructions.

All War Rooms staff were also instructed to keep their gas masks to hand at all times and to listen out for the sounding of a rattle in the corridors – the agreed warnings for such attacks.

They were also told to keep a complete change of clothes in the War Rooms, to put on in case the clothing they were wearing became contaminated.

MOCK ATTACK

Sir John Winnifrith was Assistant Secretary and Establishment Officer at the War Rooms from 1942 to 1944. Here he describes how he was asked to join the Home Guard in a mock attack on the War Rooms, which exposed weaknesses in the site's defences:

'Well, it was terribly satisfactory from the point of view of the Home Guard. We'd brought ladders with us and it so happened that the defending platoon had chosen to deploy themselves in Great George Street. This left the coast entirely clear [on the other side] and we rushed forward, got our ladders up and in no time got in through the windows. Admittedly the fact that the windows were unguarded and that there was no-one there in the rooms at the time was an accident, and if a German parachute attack or an invasion had been in the offing undoubtedly more would have been done to provide defences at this point. It was terribly satisfying for us as attackers to be marching round the corridors of the war cabinet office ready to slaughter anything in sight... I think any report of our activities would be most unlikely to have reached the ears of the Prime Minister!'

▶ Fortunately the War Rooms staff never had to act on the advice given on this sign. The closest the site came to a direct hit was in September 1940, when a bomb left a crater near the Clive Steps where the entrance to the War Rooms now stands.

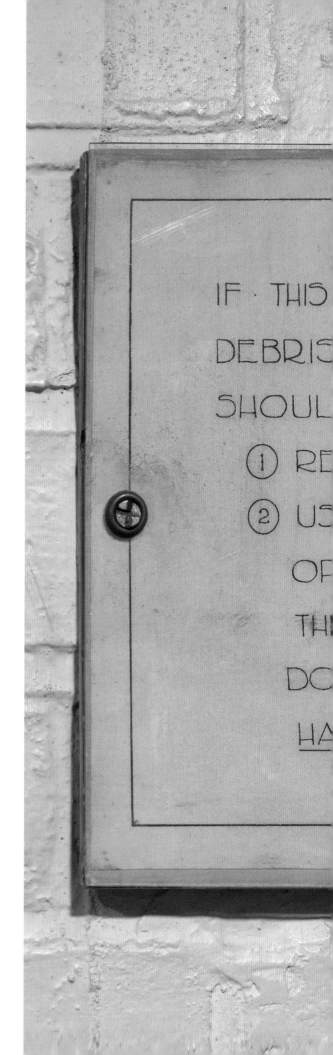

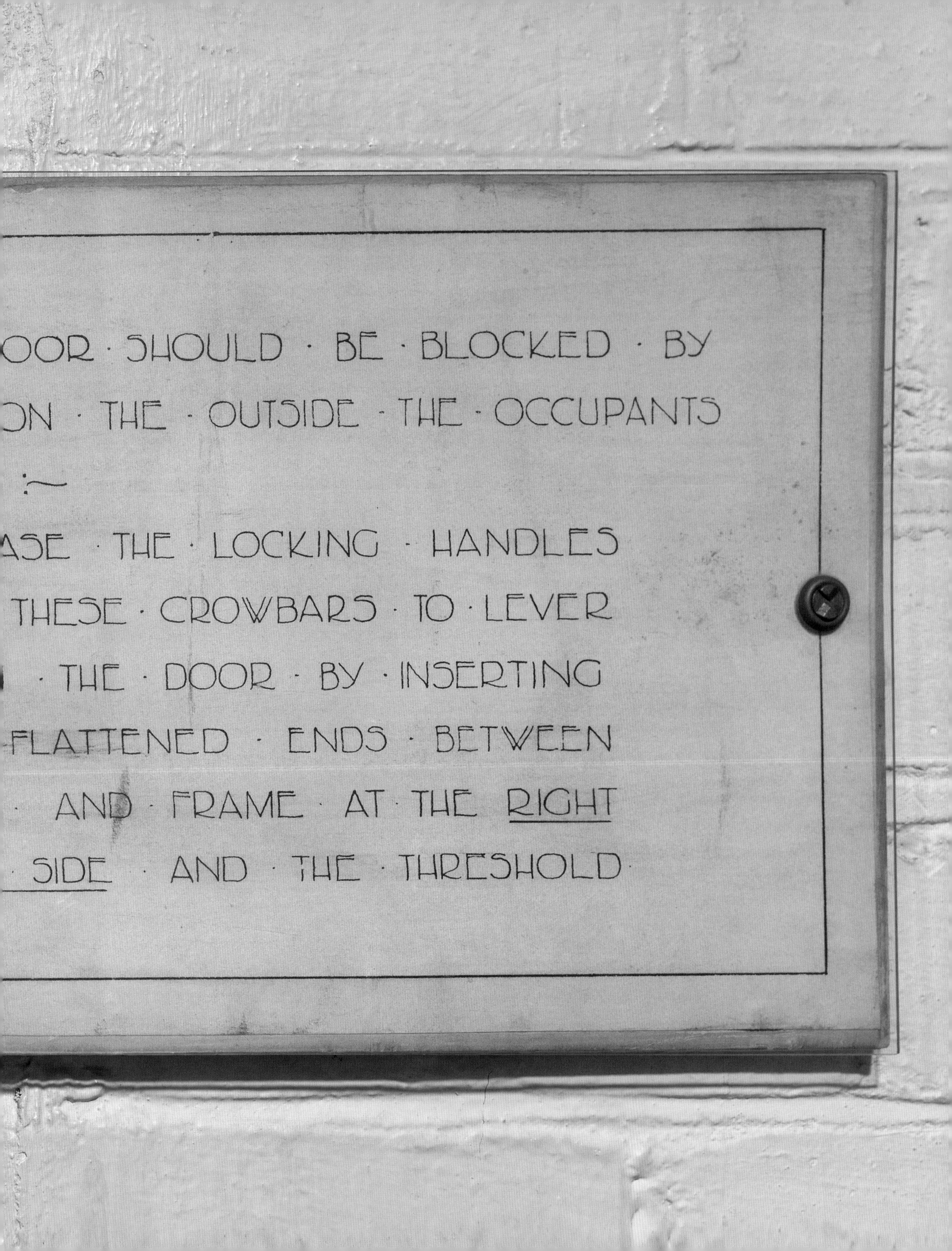

OOR · SHOULD · BE · BLOCKED · BY

ON · THE · OUTSIDE · THE · OCCUPANTS

:~

ASE · THE · LOCKING · HANDLES

THESE · CROWBARS · TO · LEVER

· THE · DOOR · BY · INSERTING

FLATTENED · ENDS · BETWEEN

AND · FRAME · AT · THE · <u>RIGHT</u>

<u>SIDE</u> · AND · THE · THRESHOLD

CHURCHILL'S ROOM

On 27 July 1940 this room was set aside for Winston Churchill. He is known to have slept overnight here only a couple of times during the war, but he used the room as an office before and after meetings with the War Cabinet or Chiefs of Staff, and he is thought to have enjoyed some of his famous afternoon naps here too. It was also the backdrop to four of his wartime radio broadcasts, using the BBC microphones arranged on his desk. The room was preserved after the war, but some of the furniture has since been rearranged to accommodate the addition of the glass wall on one side.

Churchill's bedroom was large by the standards of the War Rooms (it was originally intended to be the meeting room for the War Cabinet before another even larger room was freed up). It was also supremely well positioned next door to the Map Room, where Churchill would often drop in to catch up on the latest developments.

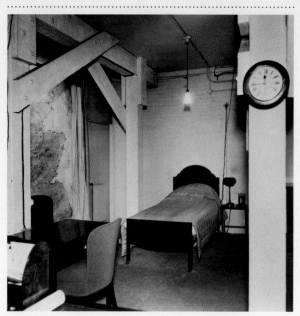
Churchill's Room photographed c.1945

THE DICTATOR

Churchill was well known for his unusual working practices. Here the Prime Minister's Private Secretary Sir John Colville recalls a scene that took place in his War Rooms bedroom in November 1940:

'I remember vividly going into his bedroom down there one evening and it was just when Neville Chamberlain died and he was dictating to Mrs Hill, one of his personal secretaries, a very moving speech, which he made the next day in the House of Commons.

And [he did] that certainly... lying flat on his bed looking, I think, not totally proper because he did rather forget who was in the room... He dictated quite a lot from that room – quite a lot of his speeches – because he liked to lie in bed and dictate.'

When Churchill became Prime Minister, he told George Rance never to let the clocks tell the wrong time. According to Leslie Hollis, Rance only failed in his job once, when the clock in the Cabinet Room stopped one evening in June 1943. Churchill was quick to take Rance to task.

Perhaps surprisingly, the bed provided for Churchill was of the standard small Civil Service type seen all over Whitehall. He is nonetheless known to have spent the night here three times.

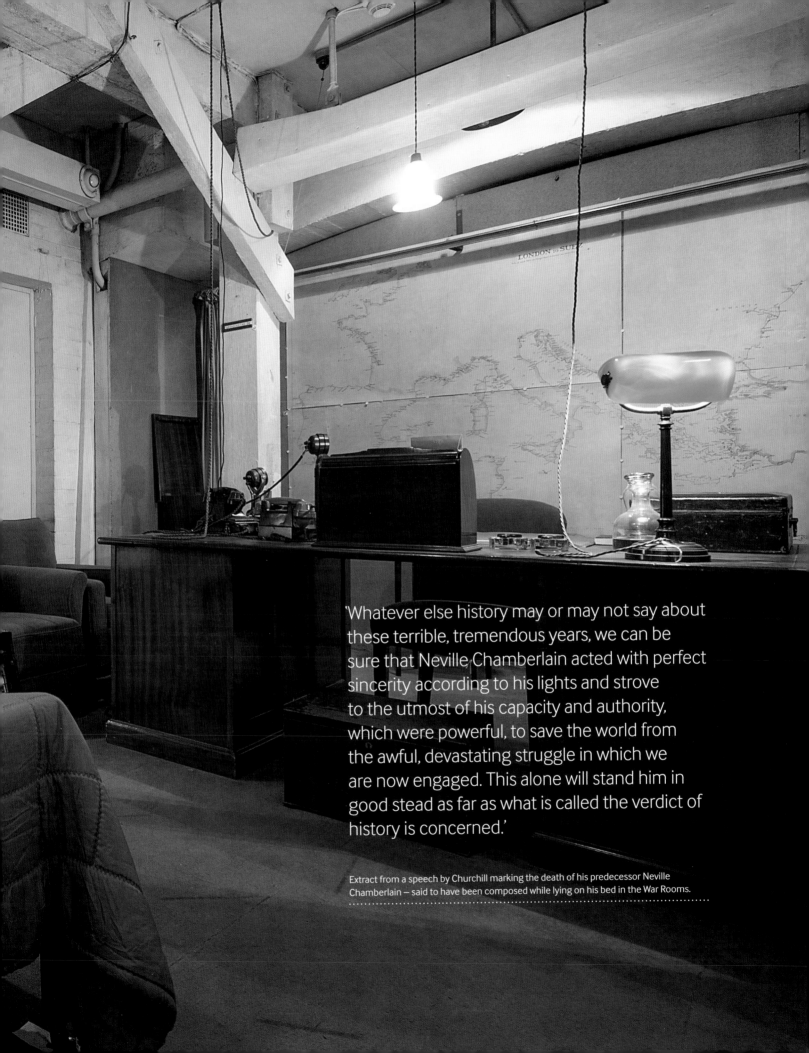

'Whatever else history may or may not say about these terrible, tremendous years, we can be sure that Neville Chamberlain acted with perfect sincerity according to his lights and strove to the utmost of his capacity and authority, which were powerful, to save the world from the awful, devastating struggle in which we are now engaged. This alone will stand him in good stead as far as what is called the verdict of history is concerned.'

Extract from a speech by Churchill marking the death of his predecessor Neville Chamberlain — said to have been composed while lying on his bed in the War Rooms.

Churchill made four speeches from his underground bedroom. A BBC technician remembers that he had a habit of slightly varying his broadcasts from the prepared text. If anyone else tried to do this, the engineer in charge was under strict instructions to throw the 'security switch' and black out the alteration. Churchill, however, was allowed to get away with it...

The desk assigned to Churchill was unusually wide. On its leather-topped surface sat a device with three buttons on it so that the Prime Minister could call on the services of his detective, butler or private secretary as required.

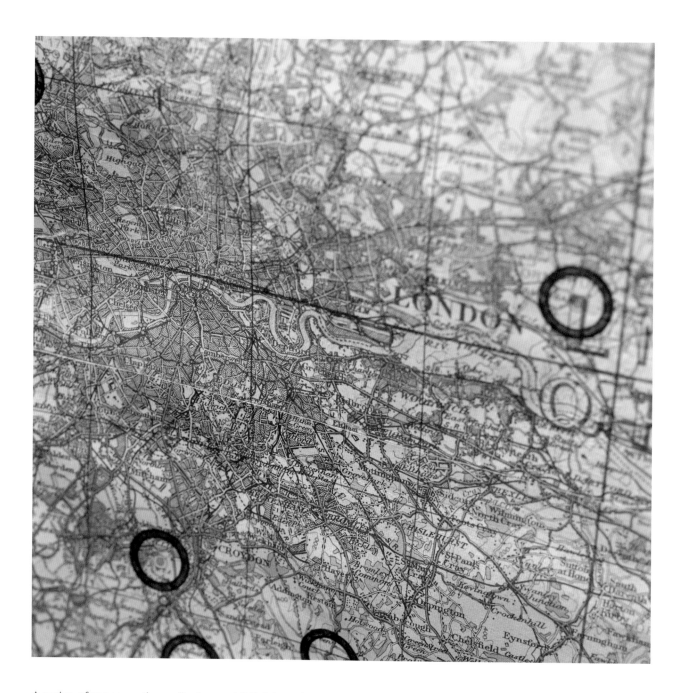

A series of maps on the walls showed Britain's main coastal and air defence installations, as well as possible landing sites for a German invasion – the Prime Minister's chief concern in the dark days of 1940. Curtains were provided so that the maps could be discreetly covered while Churchill was entertaining visitors.

Sitting within easy reach of the Prime Minister's bed was an emergency lamp in case of any electrical problem. There were also a couple of candles available on the desk, although no such loss of power ever took place.

3

THE
TIDE TURNS

June 1941 to December 1943

On 22 June 1941, the colourful bank of telephones in the Map Room – known as the 'beauty chorus' – brought dramatic news to the Cabinet War Rooms. The German Army had invaded the Soviet Union. The reports came as no surprise to the occupants of Churchill's underground bunker. Over the course of the previous few months, they had received repeated intelligence of Hitler's plans. Churchill had tried to warn Stalin as early as 3 April, and despite his long-held antipathy to Communism he was poised to welcome the Soviet Union as a new, if unlikely, ally. Talking to his private secretary John Colville the night before the invasion, he remarked that 'if Hitler invaded Hell, I would make at least a favourable reference to the devil in the House of Commons'. And in a radio address the following night, he made it clear that 'any man or state who fights against Nazidom will have our aid'.

In common with most informed observers, Churchill did not expect his new ally to fare any better against the rampant German Army than had the French, Polish, Yugoslavs, Greeks and, indeed, the British. The only fighting partner that Churchill longed to have in his corner was the United States, and he spent much of 1941 courting their support. After some negotiation, in March a 'Lend Lease' agreement was passed, through which the

US would go on to supply as much as a quarter of all Britain's munitions. And in August, he hoped to make further progress by meeting with Roosevelt in person. It was an arrangement steeped in secrecy. Roosevelt set off for a 'fishing trip' in Maine and then boarded a US cruiser to journey to Placentia Bay in Newfoundland. Churchill meanwhile travelled by his specially converted armoured train as far as Thurso in Scotland and then boarded the battleship HMS *Prince of Wales* to make a speedy Atlantic crossing.

Back in London, the staff of the War Rooms were forced to adjust to life without the Prime Minister, two of the three Chiefs of Staff and several other key advisers and aides. There could be no pause in activity; reports still had to be prepared, plans made and decisions taken. Deputies took on extra responsibilities, tasks were delegated and long-distance lines of communication were established and put to the test. It was a sign of things to come, for what seemed atypical during those two weeks in August 1941 would become commonplace in the years ahead.

Churchill returned to Britain with little of substance to show for the meeting. He was glad to have had the chance to make a personal impression on Roosevelt, but it was clear that words alone would not be enough to bring the

US into the war. Over the course of the next hundred days or so Churchill projected his usual confidence in victory – he made use of his famously ebullient 'V' sign for the first time at around this period – but the truth was that he was waiting for something to happen. On 7 December, something did.

The surprise Japanese attack on the US fleet at Pearl Harbor triggered a sudden escalation of the war. Broadcasting from the War Rooms the following evening, Churchill condemned the 'base and brutal' actions of the Japanese and warned of further dangers to come. But, leaning into the microphone on the desk of his bedroom study, he signed off his address by looking forward to a brighter future:

> In the past we had a light which flickered, in the present we have a light which flames, and in the future there will be a light which will shine calm and resplendent over all the land and all the sea!

Despite Churchill's confidence, this new phase of the war brought disaster upon disaster for Britain and its Empire. While the US fleet burned at Pearl Harbor, the Japanese were attacking British territories across the Far East by land, sea and air. On 10 December, HMS *Prince of Wales* – the battleship that had carried Churchill to Newfoundland in August – was hit by Japanese torpedoes and sunk off the coast of Malaya. It was grim news to receive as Churchill boarded her sister ship HMS *Duke of York* to journey to Washington two days later.

It was a difficult time too for the Prime Minister himself. Unknown to all but his closest aides, he suffered a heart attack during the trip to Washington and by the time he returned to Britain, he faced a vote of confidence in the House of Commons. It is not hard to understand the concerns of his fellow MPs. Almost two years into Churchill's premiership, every ocean bar the Atlantic was under enemy control, continental Europe was overrun by German troops, and the British Army had enjoyed no lasting success anywhere on the globe.

Churchill gave a powerful defence of his administration in Parliament and secured an overwhelming majority in his favour, but even he became shaken over the next few weeks as bad news continued to pour into the Map Room. There

were reverses for British troops in North Africa, and almost continual losses of territory in the Far East, with the fall of Singapore on 15 February a desperate low point. To make matters worse, the number of merchant ships being lost to Nazi submarines was getting higher and higher. Churchill later admitted that this 'U-boat peril' was the one thing that really frightened him. It is all too easy to imagine him staring in concern at the vast convoy map that dominates one wall of the Map Room and worrying about whether Britain would soon lack the capacity to stay in the war.

Since the fall of France in 1940, the only way that Britain could strike back directly at Germany was from the air, but by early 1942 it was becoming clear that the RAF's bombers did not have either the range or the accuracy to inflict serious strategic damage. Many parts of Germany were out of reach and only one in four bombs fell within five miles of its target. Behind the scenes at the War Rooms, and tabled for discussion by the Chiefs of Staff and the War Cabinet, the question was raised of how to go about exacting a more effective strategic return. The result was a decision to switch to 'area bombing', subjecting broad swathes of German cities to concentrated – and controversial – attack.

While the RAF was engaged in these deadly operations, the British Army was struggling to stand its ground in the Far East and in North Africa. News of fresh defeats and humiliations came so regularly that Churchill began to doubt whether the troops were up to the job – a fear shared by Alan Brooke, who had become the Army Chief of Staff at the end of 1941. 'If the Army cannot fight better than it is doing at present,' Brooke confided in his diary, 'we shall deserve to lose our Empire.'

The Army's performance proved especially embarrassing to Churchill during his second visit to Washington in June 1942. During one meeting in the Oval Office he was handed news of the fall of Tobruk to German troops in North Africa – news made all the more difficult to take coming, as it did, in front of Roosevelt himself. Once more Churchill found himself returning to Britain with his own future at risk. 'Now for England,' he said as he departed Washington, 'home, and a beautiful row.'

This time Parliament was debating a vote of censure about the Prime Minister's conduct of the war. He survived the vote 475 to 25, but was sorely wounded by the many critical comments made during the debate. Knowing that he needed to reverse the tide of events, Churchill took to his travels again that August, flying to Cairo, Moscow and Teheran to do whatever he could to influence the war on the ground. It was in Cairo that he decided to shake up command of the Army in North Africa, bringing in a new Commander-in-Chief, General Harold Alexander, and a new Commander of the Eighth Army, Lieutenant General William Gott.

Tragically, Gott was killed when the plane carrying him to Cairo was shot down – a reminder of the dangers facing Churchill himself on his many travels. Casting around for a suitable replacement, Churchill was persuaded by Brooke to select General Bernard Montgomery. It would prove to be an inspired decision. During the last days of October and early November 1942, British troops under Montgomery's command fought a fierce battle near the town of El Alamein and secured a significant victory. Back in London, Churchill was quick to seize upon the moment

Montgomery watches the beginning of the German retreat from El Alamein from the turret of his Grant Tank, 5 November 1942

with a typical rhetorical flourish: 'This is not the end. It is not even the beginning of the end. But it is, perhaps, the end of the beginning.'

The success at El Alamein and the almost unopposed Allied landings in North Africa on 8 November marked a turning point in the war. After three long years, Britain was able to switch its attention from defence to attack and, within a few months, Axis forces would be driven out of North Africa altogether. It was a change of focus symbolically mirrored in the War Rooms. The Advanced Headquarters of the Home Forces – so hurriedly installed there amid the fear of invasion in July 1940 – left the premises to take up new offices elsewhere. The vacated space was immediately taken up by the swelling numbers of Joint Planning and Joint Intelligence staff, whose job it was to assess and propose strategies to push the Allied cause forward. Together they formed the bulk of the occupants of the War Rooms for the rest of the war.

The Joint Planners carried out the preparatory work for every action undertaken in every theatre of the war, but they also scoped out countless operations that were never undertaken – some because they were rejected by the Chiefs of Staff, others because events rendered them obsolete. It was also their job to examine the many schemes, plans and strategies suggested by Churchill himself and, if necessary, point out their difficulties and impracticalities. This saw the Joint Planners described by the characteristically frustrated Prime Minister as epitomising 'the whole machinery of negation', but it was their industry and expertise that formed the bedrock of the Allied war effort.

The work of the intelligence section on the other hand was always of interest to Churchill, who did much to see it lay claim to an increasing amount of space in the War Rooms. In 1942, for example, Room 59 was among a number of offices made available to 'C' – the codename given to Brigadier Stewart Menzies, the wartime head of the Secret Intelligence Service. Under his direction, the Joint Intelligence staff collated and assessed enormous amounts of covertly obtained military information, including 'Ultra' – the code name given to German messages scrambled by the Enigma machine but decoded by the Government Code and Cypher School at Bletchley Park.

By this stage of the war, the concrete slab protecting the War Rooms had reached its full extent. A site originally intended to amount to no more than four or five rooms had become a complex of some 150 separate chambers, with a mile's worth of corridors criss-crossing a six-acre area. Scores of officers and administrative personnel – typists, stenographers, telephonists and secretaries – worked in this basement, with some unfortunate enough to occupy offices in the confines of the sub-basement. Leading Aircraftwoman Myra Murden was one of them, helping a team of draftsmen to create and maintain the maps needed in the Map Room. She recalls the grim conditions that they had to work in:

> The ventilator used to be burring and hurring all the time, with air coming down… I put a handkerchief over it and within an hour or two it had turned black with soot.

In the absence of any aerial threat, the War Cabinet only met in the War Rooms five times in 1942 and twice in 1943. The sight of Churchill stalking the corridors – so regularly seen during the Blitz – was also much less common. In fact, in 1943 the Prime Minister would spend almost half the year out of the country, taking with him many of the War Rooms staff. Churchill placed great store in these foreign trips. By the end of 1942, it was clear that Britain was no longer Germany's most powerful military opponent. The US had brought its unparalleled firepower and economic might to the war, and the Soviet Union had confounded all expectations by forcing a halt to what had seemed like an inexorable German advance. But Churchill was determined that neither he nor Britain would be sidelined. He saw every conference and foreign meeting as a way to exert influence on the course of the war, and he instructed his staff to prepare as assiduously as possible for each event.

These conferences were a mixed blessing for the staff of the War Rooms and the No 10 Annexe. Apart from all the preparatory work, there was the headache of deciding who should go, who should stay behind and how to ensure that this division of resources didn't impact on the effective direction of the war. At first it was deemed impossible for civilian women to be involved – due to the restrictions on females boarding Royal Navy ships and the discomfort of high altitude military air travel. This meant that the many

Winston Churchill stands on the battlement of the Citadel in Quebec during the Quebec Conference, Canada, August 1943

secretaries and personal assistants at work in London were excluded from the travelling party – much to their frustration. It was only from May 1943 onwards that the rules were changed, which meant that a select few were able to leave the austerity of Britain behind and sample the delights of Washington, Quebec, Cairo, Teheran and Tunis before the year was out.

The Prime Minister began 1943 by travelling to an Allied conference in Casablanca. It came at a key moment in the war. The British were buoyed by their success at El Alamein and the Soviets were on the verge of forcing a German surrender at Stalingrad. High on the agenda was the question of when the western Allies would launch an invasion of northern France, opening up the 'Second Front', which the Soviets hoped would draw German strength away from the East. The Americans agreed that such a strategy was the most direct way to strike at Germany, but the British had other ideas. Churchill believed it made more sense to move against the Germans in North Africa and the Mediterranean, and he arrived at the conference

with a large well-prepared entourage, ready to carry the day. He succeeded. Plans for the invasion of France were shelved and the focus turned instead to a push through North Africa, then Sicily in July and finally mainland Italy in September.

Churchill's travels were often undertaken in uncomfortable conditions, flying at altitude or buffeted by strong seas, and they took a toll on the Prime Minister's health. On his return from Casablanca in February 1943, he suffered a bout of pneumonia that saw him confined to his bed in the No 10 Annexe. And he ended the year in Tunis with another bout of pneumonia, spending a combined total of 31 days in his sickbed during the year.

Life in the War Rooms continued at pace even when Churchill and his entourage were out of the country. In fact, the workload was often increased when the many international conferences and meetings generated demand for yet more briefing documents, memos, reports and plans. As they hurried about their duties, some staff may have noticed workmen coming and going in the main corridor just along from the Map Room. They were fitting out a store room for some as yet unknown purpose – although the addition of a new door with a lavatory-style lock sparked a rumour that Churchill had been given the luxury of a private flushing toilet. In fact, the room had been adapted in the utmost secrecy to house a secure radio-telephone link between the Prime Minister and the President of the United States. The equipment in this Transatlantic Telephone Room – and a huge scrambling unit stored beneath Selfridges department store – made it impossible for the Germans to listen in to or decipher any conversation between the two leaders.

The hotline between London and Washington became operational in August 1943, at which point Churchill was in Quebec holding talks with the President in person. It was at the Quebec conference that a date was finally set for the invasion of north-west France. Churchill was still far from sure that this was the correct strategy, but in the months since Casablanca the US had become the more senior partner on the ground in Europe and British influence on events was waning. The date set for the landings was May 1944. Back in the War Rooms, preparations for Operation Overlord shifted up several gears. D-Day was approaching.

THE CHURCHILL SUITE

Early in 1941, as the Blitz raged on, the Cabinet War Rooms were expanded to include rooms for the private use of the Prime Minister and his wife. As it turned out, the worst of the bombing raids had passed by the time the rooms were ready, and little is known about how often they were used – if at all – for the remainder of the war. When in London, the Prime Minister and Mrs Churchill preferred to live in the No 10 Annexe – a set of rooms reserved for them in the building above the War Rooms.

After the war, this section of the War Rooms was stripped out and fell into disrepair. Its restoration required a combination of ingenuity and persistence from IWM's staff.

The sink, sump and pump displayed in the kitchen were found in a neglected corner of the Treasury Building. The hand-operated pump was used to remove waste water and force it back up to surface level (the underground kitchen had to operate without proper plumbing or gas).

The decision to create a suite of rooms underground for the Churchills was prompted when a bomb on 14 October 1940 destroyed the kitchen at 10 Downing Street. Just moments before the blast, Churchill had been standing in the kitchen persuading his chef, Georgina Landemare, to take shelter in the building's basement. Mrs Landemare duly survived the blast and would go on to make use of this new kitchen in the War Rooms as well as one in the No 10 Annexe. A number of the pots, pans and utensils in the kitchen were given to the museum by the granddaughter of Mrs Landemare. Churchill's cook had been allowed to keep them when she retired from their service in 1954 at the age of 72.

Mary Churchill pictured with her father onboard HMS *Duke of York*, December 1941.

MARY CHURCHILL'S EXPERIENCE

The Prime Minister's daugher, Mary Churchill, sometimes made use of her mother's bedroom in the War Rooms when on leave from the Auxiliary Territorial Service. It is not an experience that she remembered fondly:

'When I stayed I was allotted one of the emergency bedrooms in the Cabinet War Rooms complex down below the Annexe flat; my clothes, however, were kept (mostly in my suitcase) in a bathroom used by the women secretaries (which cannot have been convenient for them). At night, I would get into my nightclothes there and make my way 'down below'. Passing the sentry on duty at the Annexe front door on my way up and down in my dressing gown and tin hat was a perpetual source of humiliation to me, as I imagined he must think I was the only 'windy' one in the family!'

▲ For more than forty years the sign for Clementine Churchill's room was in the possession of American serviceman Lieutenant Ray Edghill. It was Edghill's job to set up the connection in the Transatlantic Telephone Room whenever a call was scheduled between Churchill and the US President. During one visit to the War Rooms in 1945, the American noticed the plaque sticking up out of a bin and decided to save it for posterity. In the months before the museum was opened in 1984, he contacted IWM and arranged for it to be returned.

▶ Mrs Churchill's room is notable for the absence of a desk and the apparent attempts to soften the spartan accommodation with items such as an armchair, with its softer fabric and upholstery. It is unlikely that Mrs Churchill herself had any hand in the layout of the room, but she did take a guiding interest in the furnishing of the No 10 Annexe above, painting the walls, hanging pictures and using much of the couple's own furniture. Her husband couldn't see the point of taking such trouble, but he later admitted that she had done a good job.

▼ A set of photographs of the War Rooms taken in 1946, including this one of Mrs Churchill's bedroom, later proved vital to the restoration process. In 1983 IWM's curators also discovered a box of objects from Mrs Churchill's bedroom that had remained unopened since the war. The sheets and pillowcases that it contained had disintegrated, but the black Bakelite telephone and white porcelain water jugs had survived and have since been restored to their old positions.

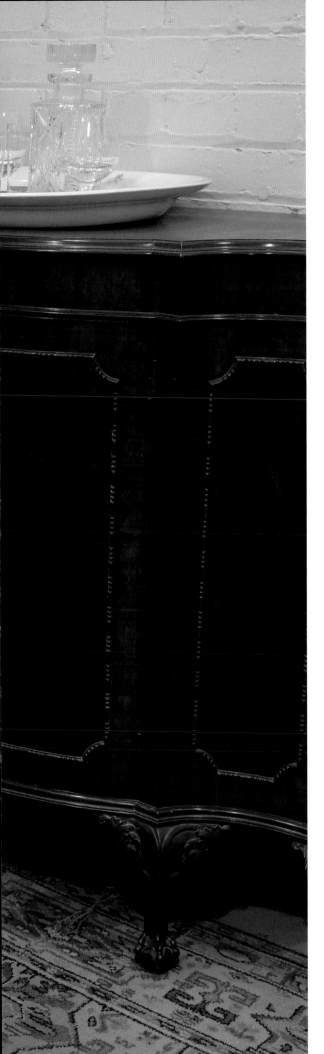

It is unlikely that the Churchills ever ate a meal in the dining room reserved for their use. It is arguably the most incongruous room in the whole underground complex, with its well-appointed furniture standing in contrast to the whitewashed brick walls.

The table and sideboard in the dining room are the originals that furnished the room in wartime.

CHURCHILL'S ENTOURAGE

When the corridor that leads to the Churchill Suite was opened up in spring 1941, several other rooms were also made available for use. Some were assigned to members of Churchill's personal staff, such as his bodyguards, his aide-de-camp Commander Charles 'Tommy' Thompson, his Parliamentary Private Secretary Brigadier George Harvie-Watt, and the head of his secretarial pool Margaret Stenhouse. Others were given to key members of his inner circle, such as his intelligence adviser Major Desmond Morton and his close friend and Minister of Information Brendan Bracken. Some of these rooms have been restored for viewing today.

Brendan Bracken was one of Churchill's closest confidants. A fellow Conservative MP, he acted as Churchill's Parliamentary Private Secretary until 1941, when he was appointed Minister of Information — a role he carried out with great success. This set of pyjamas is on display in Bracken's room. Like Desmond Morton and Churchill's scientific adviser Frederick Lindemann, Bracken was unmarried and had plenty of time to devote to the Prime Minister. In Bracken's case, this does not seem to have endeared him to Mrs Churchill, who is said to have mistrusted his influence on her husband.

Naval officer Commander Charles 'Tommy' Thompson was the Prime Minister's aide-de-camp — a kind of military personal assistant. He was rarely seen away from Churchill's side during the war, so it is no surprise that he was given emergency accommodation in the War Rooms (shown above is a razor on display in Thompson's room). One of Thompson's duties involved making travel arrangements for Churchill's entourage and baggage — this was no mean feat considering how unpredictable Churchill's movements could be.

It is unknown how often – if at all – Commander Thompson made use of his underground bedroom/study. Given the Prime Minister's preference for staying above ground, it is likely that Thompson chose to do the same.

As Prime Minister, Churchill was given a two-man Special Branch protection team. The senior of the two bodyguards was Detective Walter H Thompson, who had been assigned to protect Churchill between 1921 and 1935 before retiring in 1936. On 22 August 1939 Thompson was working in the family grocer's shop when he received a telegram from Churchill. 'Meet me Croydon Airport 4.30pm Wednesday,' it read. Thompson was back on the job.

The room for Churchill's detectives was fitted with bunk-beds to accommodate the two men who alternated on bodyguard duty. A stretcher was on stand-by to carry the Prime Minister in case he was injured in the War Rooms.

After the war, Walter Thompson revealed that Churchill was determined to go down fighting. Thompson was ordered to keep a .45 Colt pistol fully loaded for the Prime Minister's use. 'He intended to use every bullet but one on the enemy,' wrote the detective. 'The last one he saved for himself.'

▲ The bell displayed on the wall was found in another government building and added to the room during its restoration. It is actually a division bell, one of hundreds in the buildings immediately around Parliament, which were used to alert MPs whenever a vote was imminent.

◄ This asbestos cloth dispenser and the nearby boxes of anti-louse powder are the same as were actually present in this room in August 1945.

During the inter-war years, Major Desmond Morton worked in military intelligence – thanks to the intervention of Churchill, when he was Secretary of State for War between 1919 and 1922. In the 1930s, when Churchill was out of favour, Morton became a valued member of his inner circle, keeping him in the loop on military and intelligence matters. It was a role he would continue to fulfil on a more official basis during the war.

There were no washing facilities available at basement level, so each bedroom contained a washing jug and bowl for the occupant's use. Seen here are those on display in Major Morton's room.

Churchill is seen with Detective Thompson, August 1940

A RELUCTANT GUEST

A few years after the war Thompson wrote an account of his time as the Prime Minister's bodyguard. Here he recalls how hard it was to persuade Churchill to stay overnight in the War Rooms:

'Mr Churchill preferred sleeping and working in his suite on a floor above. But I remember on one occasion Mrs Churchill made him promise to go down below when the raid started, and requested me to see that he carried out her wishes. So when I made my usual report to him about the strength of the enemy, he gathered up his papers and we marched down to the basement room. I was mystified by the docility with which he went downstairs and noticed with some apprehension the cynical smile on his face. When I had seen him into bed and arranged everything ready for him at the bedside I went to turn out the light.

'"Leave it on, Thompson", said the Old Man. I retired to my own room, but I did not undress. Sure enough, not long afterwards, Mr Churchill rang his bell. I tapped at the door and went in. He had put on a dressing gown and was gathering up his papers. "Well, Thompson, I have kept my word," he said with a chuckle. "I came downstairs to go to bed. Now I am going upstairs to sleep!"'

SWITCHBOARD

Many of the rooms in Churchill's bunker performed a variety of roles during the war. Room 60 Right was originally used by typists before serving as a switchboard from the summer of 1940 through to at least spring 1941. Later in the war, as more space became available elsewhere in the basement, it was reserved as emergency accommodation, and by the end of the war it had become an office for the Royal Marine guards. Today it has been restored to reflect the role that it carried out as home to the War Rooms switchboard.

Switchboard operators in the War Rooms – and at places like the Post Office, hospitals and airfields – were given specially adapted gas masks that would allow them to continue their work even in the event of a gas attack. Fortunately they were only ever put to use in drills.

Throughout the darkest days of the Blitz, shifts of switchboard operators would work, two at a time, in this room at all hours of the day and night. It was their job to connect the War Rooms to the outside world.

Until the spring of 1941 space in the War Rooms was extremely hard to come by, meaning that two or three typists were also crammed in beside the switchboard operators. It was only when the protective concrete slab was expanded to cover more of the basement rooms that the pressure eased. One of the new rooms became a new, and much bigger, switchboard facility.

▲ The switchboard operators and typists in Room 60 Right were all civilian women. During the Blitz, many of them remained underground day and night, working here and sleeping between shifts in the dock.

◀ One of the operators who worked at this switchboard remembers that there was no such thing as an emergency call — not because there were no emergencies, but because every single call was treated as urgent.

TYPISTS

From July 1940 to July 1941, Room 60A was occupied by the typing pool for the Joint Planning Staff. It was later partitioned to form two smaller emergency bedrooms, but has now been restored to reflect the period of the war in which it saw the most sustained activity.

Each typist worked beneath a green-shaded lamp slung low from the ceiling. When interviewed by IWM historians during the restoration of the War Rooms one of the typists, Margaret d'Arcy (née Sutherland), described how they would sometimes stick paper over the underside of the lamps to reduce the intensity of the light.

During the Blitz this room was in use 24 hours a day. It was furnished with six standard typing desks and six swivel chairs to accommodate the number of typists who worked on each shift. Against the walls were stacked six single mattresses so that the women would have somewhere safe to sleep during the raids.

The typists in the War Rooms couldn't help but read the documents that crossed their desks. One woman is said to have come across the name of her boyfriend's ship. It had been sunk with the loss of all hands.

OFFICES OF THE WAR CABINET
GREAT GEORGE STREET, S.W.1

Reference No.
1/C/1095

20th July, 1943.

Dear Madam,

I am authorised, subject to satisfactory references being received, to offer you an appointment as a Temporary Shorthand Typist Grade II in this Office; and subject to one month's probation.

The wages attached to the post are 47/- plus 13/6 war bonus per week, for a minimum attendance of 44 hours per week, and are subject to statutory deductions in respect of National Health and Unemployment Insurance.

Sick and Annual Leave are authorised in accordance with the attached statement.

The appointment will be a temporary one for the war period, subject to one week's notice in writing on either side.

If you are willing to accept this appointment will you please let me know, and report to me at the above address, ready to commence your duties, at 9.30 a.m. on Monday, 26th July, 1943.

Yours faithfully,

Chief Clerk.

▲ Demand for administrative support at the War Rooms was always high, meaning that letters like this one were probably sent out quite frequently. This rare surviving example is lodged in IWM's archives.

▲ It was the job of the typing pool to produce accurate versions of all the handwritten minutes and reports generated by the Joint Planning Staff. They worked using Imperial typewriters like this one, producing one top copy and two carbon copies of each sheet.

War Rooms staff had helmets and whistles ready for use in case the site was hit during an air raid. The whistle could be used to attract attention or sound a warning.

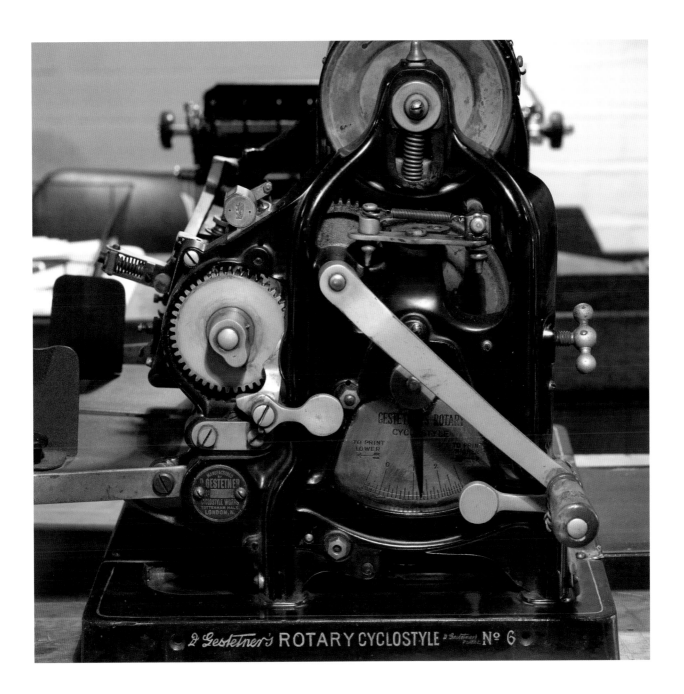

When more copies of a document were needed, a stencil was prepared for use in a Gestetner copier like this one. The stencil was put in place, the ink readied and paper was wound through the machine using a hand-operated crank. It was a laborious but essential process.

THE TRANSATLANTIC TELEPHONE ROOM

In the first few years of the war, transatlantic conversations between the Prime Minister and the US President were conducted via a radio-telephone link known to be vulnerable to enemy eavesdropping. To ensure secrecy, censors had to be employed to listen in to every conversation and cut the line whenever a forbidden subject was mentioned. In the summer of 1943, it was agreed that a new system should be used, which would encrypt the conversation so that it could no longer be deciphered by enemy spies. Work duly began to transform a store cupboard in the War Rooms to become one end of this top secret hotline.

The system used for the transatlantic telephone link was designed by Bell Telephone Laboratories in the US. Codenamed 'Sigsaly' and sometimes referred to as the 'X system' or 'X-Ray', it was considered so valuable by the Americans that they were reluctant to share any of its workings with the British. In the end it was agreed that the machinery should be checked for its effectiveness by British codebreaking pioneer Alan Turing. Once he gave his blessing, work began in earnest and the system was ready for use by Churchill from August 1943.

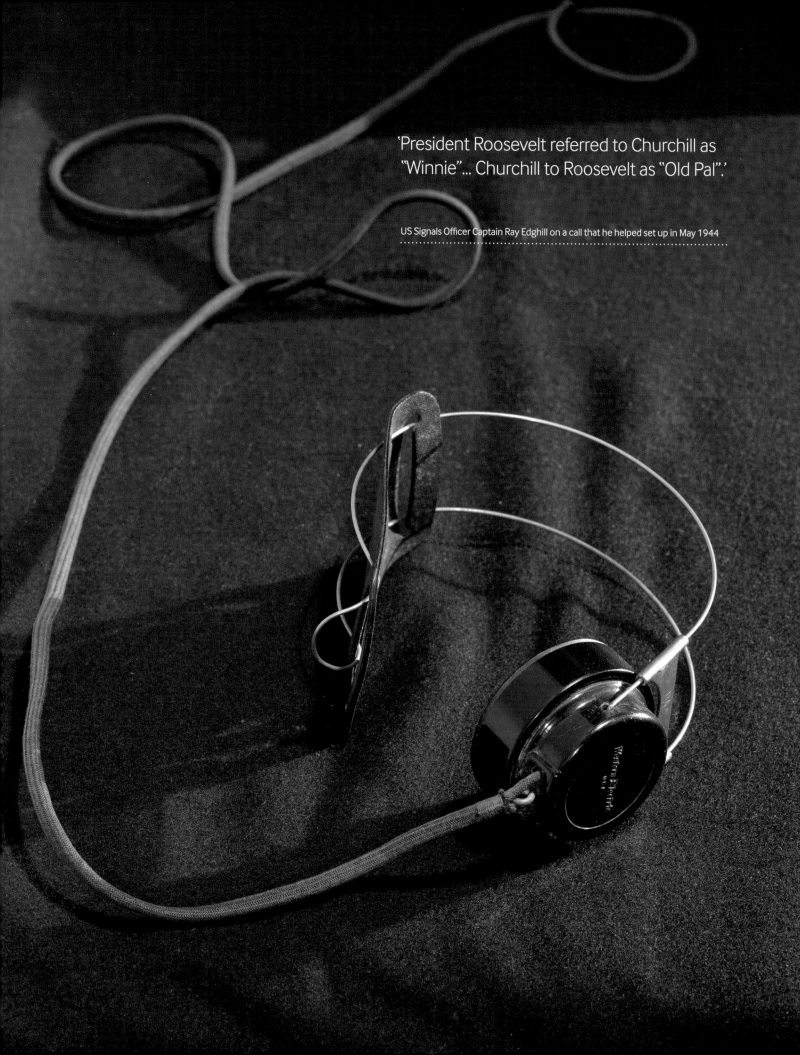

'President Roosevelt referred to Churchill as "Winnie"... Churchill to Roosevelt as "Old Pal".'

US Signals Officer Captain Ray Edghill on a call that he helped set up in May 1944

▶ The clock in the telephone room sported two black hands to indicate London time, and two red ones to show the equivalent time in Washington. According to the stipulations of the Americans, calls had to be pre-booked an hour in advance and could only be made between the hours of 2pm and 8pm. This was hardly designed to fit in comfortably with the peculiarities of Churchill's daily schedule, so it is perhaps unsurprising that he did not make use of the system until April 1944.

◀ Churchill's Personal Secretary used this headset to listen in to the conversation in order to take notes. The presence of two people in the narrow confines of the room must have added to its claustrophobic atmosphere.

▶ Sigsaly was designed to allow senior US personnel to talk in secrecy between the UK and the USA. The machinery required to make it work was installed in three large rooms below Selfridges department store in the West End. When it was decided to extend this capability to the War Rooms, a cable was run from Selfridges to this small intermediate scrambling machine in the corner of the Transatlantic Telephone Room.

When Churchill spoke into the ordinary looking phone handset, his words were immediately scrambled by the machine in the corner of the room. This partially enciphered signal was then transmitted to the Selfridges machinery, where it was fully enciphered and sent by radio to Washington. There it was received and decoded by the same equipment.

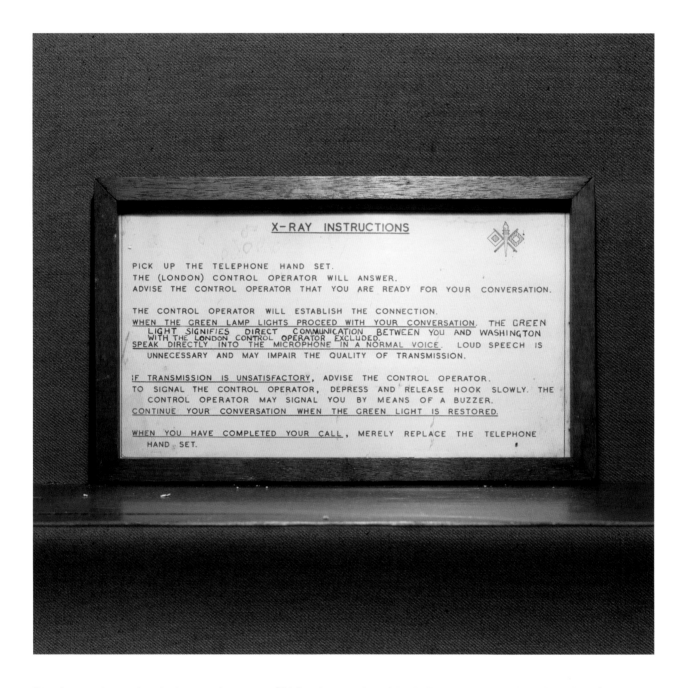

The frame above the desk contains a set of 'X-Ray Instructions', including a warning that shouting down the phone line was likely to impair the quality of transmission. The system could have other peculiar effects on a person's voice. On one occasion, it is said that President Roosevelt couldn't help but laugh on hearing Churchill speak down the line. Apparently the bulldog British Prime Minister sounded remarkably like cartoon character Donald Duck.

Only a few of the War Rooms staff were aware of the plans to create the Transatlantic Telephone Room. All they knew was that an old store cupboard was being readied for some new purpose. When a new door was fitted, complete with a lavatory-style lock, the purpose appeared to become clear – Churchill must have been given the luxury of his own private flushing toilet.

4

THE FINAL PUSH

January 1944 to August 1945

In spring 1944 Prime Minister Winston Churchill set aside his misgivings about the invasion of north-west France. He threw himself into the preparations, involving himself deeply in the work of the many Joint Planning and Joint Intelligence committees set up in the War Rooms to cover every aspect of the operation. He was characteristically interested in some of the more ingenious aspects of the landings: the floating Mulberry Harbours designed to transform the beaches into efficient entry points for troops and materiel; the deception schemes employed to divert German attention from the landing sites; and the series of modified armoured vehicles, known as 'funnies', that saw ordinary tanks become beach-combing minesweepers or flame-throwers.

As this work continued, London once more became subject to bombing raids in a 'Little Blitz' that began on 21 January and continued sporadically until 19 April. On 20 February bombs fell just yards away from the War Rooms, hitting Horse Guards Parade and St James's Park and causing damage to 10 Downing Street. Writing about the raids in his diary, Churchill's private secretary John Colville noted that London seemed to react with less ebullience than it had in 1940 and 1941. Churchill too seems to have struggled during this period, with Alan Brooke describing him as 'losing ground rapidly' and

'desperately tired' following a Chiefs of Staff meeting in March. But far from being the cause of the Prime Minister's travails, the bombing raids seem almost to have had an energising effect on him. One of the officers in the No 10 Annexe remembers how he would 'have his coat and tin hat got ready so that as soon as the guns opened fire he might proceed to the roof of the building to get a better view'.

Always keen to show off his underground facility, Churchill invited the US Chiefs of Staff and General Eisenhower – the Supreme Commander of the Allied forces – to meet with him in the War Rooms. The Map Room was of course the highlight of the tour, while Churchill's bedroom study next door provided somewhere more informal to sit after a lengthy conference. In April the Prime Minister also made use of the Transatlantic Telephone Room for the first time – as US telecommunications engineer Stephen Geis described many years later in conversation with IWM historians. Geis recalls that he stopped on his way to the War Rooms to buy the best cigar he could in case he met Churchill in person. 'Sure enough the Prime Minister, dressed in his boiler suit, came in... He took the cigar and I stepped outside... It was the thrill of my military experience.'

Throughout this period the date set for the landings was, of course, a fiercely guarded secret but it was one necessarily known to many of the staff at the War Rooms, from the officers planning the operation to the stenographers and typists beavering away on all the associated reports, minutes and briefing papers. 'Many of us knew the date of "D-Day" from the hour "Operation Overlord" was first mentioned,' said Joan Bright, who was personal assistant to General Ismay. The need for secrecy was hammered home to all staff early in the war, with one shorthand typist remembering how a colleague was led away in tears by two men she assumed were detectives. It was a message that seems to have got through, with many former staff concealing their wartime activities even from their families for decades to come.

One especially well-kept secret was Churchill's desire to be present in person at the D-Day landings – which had now been put back to the first week of June. Towards the end of May the Prime Minister informed the Admiralty that he intended to witness the operation first-hand from the decks of HMS *Belfast* – the cruiser given the honour of firing the opening shots of D-Day (now a branch of IWM moored on the Thames). The idea of Britain's wartime leader placing himself in such danger was quite clearly preposterous, but it wasn't until King George VI intervened in two separate letters – the second dated as late as 4 June – that Churchill agreed to back down.

Two days later at 5.27am HMS *Belfast* duly began bombarding one of the beaches chosen for the landings – although another trigger-happy ship stole the honour of the first shot by about a minute. Churchill eventually made it to the Normandy coast on board the destroyer HMS *Kelvin* on 12 June, and made sure that the ship joined in with the bombardment of German positions while he was on the bridge. By that stage Allied troops had secured a firm foothold along the coastline and the scene was set for a bitter struggle south and eastwards towards Germany.

Churchill was back in London on 13 June – in time to receive reports of 'flying bombs' appearing in the skies above south-east England. This was the first use by Germany of its *Vergeltungswaffen* or 'revenge weapons', and as wave after wave of 'V1s' continued to swarm over the Channel at any hour of the day or night, the staff of the War Rooms were once more glad of the protection afforded by their underground location. Five days later David Lee, an officer in the Joint Planning section, was working at his desk when the monotonous thrum of the ventilation fans was suddenly shattered.

It was a Sunday morning...and at eleven o'clock there was an appalling explosion. We were working down there in our office and our first thought was that we'd been hit. Well, it was the bomb that fell on the Guards Chapel about two to three hundred yards down Birdcage Walk in the middle of the morning service. A lot of people were killed and what happened was the force of the explosion travelled underground and rocked us about. It didn't do any damage – we were too far away – but I remember that incident very well.

The next day the meeting of the War Cabinet was held in the shelter of the War Rooms for the first time that year. It would become a regular haunt for Churchill, his ministers and his Chiefs of Staff throughout the rest of June, July and August, until 9 September when the threat posed by the V1s began to dwindle in the face of more effective defence measures.

By this stage, the walls of the Map Room were showing US troops on the western border of Germany, Soviet troops advancing into German territory in the east and a newly liberated Paris back in the hands of the Free French forces. Churchill, meanwhile, was in Quebec for a second bilateral conference with the Americans. Little of note was achieved at the meeting, where both sides appeared to steer clear of their strategic differences. The Americans were content to spend time massing their troops ahead of what they hoped would be a decisive offensive against the centre of the German lines. The British, on the other hand, were keen to push into Germany quickly so that they could meet the Russian forces as far east as possible and so limit the advance of Communism across the Continent.

Churchill returned to Britain on 26 September, by which time London was facing a new threat in the form of the V2 rocket – the world's first ballistic missile. Intelligence reports about these deadly new weapons had started to filter through to the War Rooms in 1943, and they were on the agenda at both meetings of the War Cabinet held underground that year. Concern about their destructive potential led to renewed calls for the War Rooms to be moved away from the capital, but Churchill once more refused to budge unless London suffered a scale of attack far worse than anything experienced to date.

The number of V2 rockets launched against London steadily increased, until on 9 January 1945 the War Cabinet was once more forced to meet underground. There it would largely stay until 28 March, when most of the V2 launching sites had been overrun by the advancing Allied forces. That meeting of the War Cabinet was the 115th to be held underground during the war – out of a total of 1,188 held between September 1939 and July 1945. It also turned out to be the last.

Much of the attention of the War Cabinet at this time was focussed on the shape of the post-war world. This too was the main subject for discussion by the 'Big Three' – Churchill, Roosevelt and Stalin – at the Yalta Conference held in February 1945. Some 750 ministers, officers and support staff set out from London for the Crimea. Most travelled by ship but the Prime Minister, Chiefs of Staff and senior officers went by three planes that took off from RAF Northolt on 29 January. Only two of the planes, including the one carrying Churchill, made it to the stop-off point on Malta. The third overshot the island and crashed into the sea, killing 14 of the 19 passengers on-board. It was shocking news for the close-knit community of the War Rooms, where several of

Winston Churchill, Franklin D Roosevelt and Joseph Stalin sit for photographs during the Yalta Conference in February 1945

the victims, including one Map Room officer, were well known. It was also another grim reminder of the dangers that Churchill faced on his many wartime journeys.

The Yalta Conference itself turned out to be a gloomy affair for the British delegation, which once again found itself sidelined by the two larger superpowers. Churchill himself couldn't wait to leave, stopping off in Athens, Alexandria and Cairo before flying home on what would be his last long-distance journey of the war. It was also the last time he would see President Roosevelt, who died after a prolonged decline in health on 12 April.

London in April 1945 was a city transformed. The terrors of the V-weapon offensive were over, and when staff emerged from the War Rooms at the end of a long day's shift they were greeted by street lamps lit for the first time in five years. Berlin, in contrast, was a city on the verge of ruin. Hitler was locked in his own bunker, trapped by bombing raids and Allied armies converging from east and west. It was a complex originally designed as a temporary air raid shelter for the Führer, but expanded during the war to include facilities such as a Map Room, bedrooms, offices and switchboard. It was here in his study that Hitler committed suicide on 30 April.

Just over a week later, on 8 May, the Allies declared Victory in Europe Day, sparking huge celebrations in central London. Shorthand typist Ilene Hutchinson remembers how she and other War Rooms staff climbed on to the rooftop to see what was going on:

> We got up onto the roof of the office and we managed to walk right along to… the Home Office, I think, but on the roof… We watched all the crowds, thousands and thousands and thousands. There was hardly a hair's breadth between them. They just held hands… and it was amazing. And then, when Mr Churchill appeared in this open limousine, he had his hat in one hand, cigar in the other and he was just standing waving them both and of course they went mad. Absolute frenzy there was… Then I had to go back to work!

Before this early evening appearance in Whitehall, Churchill had lunched with the King, delivered a broadcast to the nation, spoken in the House of Commons, attended a service of thanksgiving, spent an hour in the smoking room at Parliament and then returned to Buckingham Palace with the War Cabinet and Chiefs of Staff for royal congratulations. It was a day of great public celebration, but in private his morale was low. The war against Japan still needed to be won, the shape of post-war Europe was in the balance, Britain's coffers were empty and serious cracks were beginning to appear in his coalition government. He took to spending much more time 'working in bed', and became so infirm that he had to be carried up and down to the War Rooms on a wooden chair by the Royal Marines.

His visits to the War Rooms were now solely made to use the Transatlantic Telephone Room and to drop into the Map Room to catch up with progress in the war against Japan. The other rooms in the underground complex were already being vacated – with staff no longer needing the protection of a concrete slab and steel girders above their heads. Even for those left behind, including the Joint Planners working on the continuing war in the Far East, thoughts were beginning to turn to life after the war – to new careers, relationships and homes.

Churchill's position in the post-war world was also uncertain. He had hoped to hold his coalition government together until Japan was defeated, but the Labour Party disagreed. By 12 June, the Prime Minister bowed to the inevitable. Parliament was dissolved and a general election – the first in a decade – was set for 5 July. Churchill fought a vigorous campaign and, when the polls closed, he was confident of victory. The result, however, would not be announced until 26 July to allow time for millions of votes to come in from troops stationed abroad.

In the meantime, Churchill was able to take a short holiday in the south of France before his attention switched to the Potsdam Conference scheduled for 17 July. The city of Potsdam lies just outside Berlin, so the trip to Germany gave Churchill and his entourage the chance to visit the capital of the ruined Third Reich. Dressed in military uniform, the British leader picked his way through the rubble above Hitler's bunker. Perhaps his mind went back to the words he growled out almost five years earlier, on the day he first entered his own War Rooms as Prime Minister: 'If the invasion takes place,' he had said, 'that's

Winston Churchill makes a speech in Uxbridge, Middlesex, during the general election campaign, 27 June 1945

where I'll sit – in that chair. And I'll sit there until either the Germans are driven back – or they carry me out dead.' How the tables had been turned.

Many of Churchill's staff also found their thoughts wandering. Amid the euphoria of victory came a depression so commonly felt that it was given its own name – the Potsdam Blues. For some the trigger was the sight of defeated Germans in 'pathetic groups trudging wearily along in search of wood for fuel'. For others it was the smell of 'decayed death' that seemed to permeate the bombed out ruins. There was also a growing understanding that an extraordinary passage of their lives was closing. Securing victory was merely the turning of the page to a new and undoubtedly much less exciting chapter.

A few days into the conference, Churchill flew back to be on the spot for the announcement of the election result, a little less sure of the outcome than he had been just weeks earlier. Few among his entourage saw anything to worry about; one was confident enough to leave most of

his baggage behind in the expectation of a swift return. He was soon making arrangements to have it sent back. Labour had won a landslide victory; the electorate deciding that the country's social problems required a more progressive set of solutions than the Conservatives could offer.

Churchill was disconsolate, spending the day of the announcement locked away in the No 10 Annexe above the War Rooms. He emerged shortly before 7 o'clock in the evening to go to Buckingham Palace to tender his resignation. The following day he bid a succession of farewells to the Cabinet, his Chiefs of Staff and to the many men and women who had served him so faithfully above and below ground in that anonymous building on Great George Street. Alan Brooke, the army chief with whom Churchill had clashed so often throughout the war, later wrote in his diary: 'It was a very sad and very moving little meeting at which I found myself unable to say much for fear of breaking down.' He ended with an encomium to the outgoing leader: 'I thank God that I was given an opportunity of working alongside of such a man, and of having my eyes opened to the fact that occasionally such supermen exist on this earth.'

As these scenes played out in the No 10 Annexe, the staff in the War Rooms continued to update their maps, plotting out the gains of territory across the Pacific, and the bombing raids over the Japanese mainland. But even in the Map Room, officers were beginning to move on. On 3 August, Ismay, who had set the creation of the War Rooms in motion, told Wing Commander John Heagerty, one of the Map Room duty officers: 'It is very sad to realise that my old friends in the Map Room are leaving one by one, and that what was once a haunt of intense interest and great friendliness will be merely an empty shell.'

In the coming days the phones in the Map Room rang to bring news of the atom bombs dropped over Hiroshima and Nagasaki. Then came talk of a Japanese surrender, which duly came on 14 August. The following day, the officers on duty in the Map Room gathered up their possessions, exchanged congratulations and made ready to head out into the summer sunshine. The last man to leave paused at the door and reached for a switch. For the first time in six years, the lights in the Map Room were turned off. The war was over.

EVERYDAY
LIFE

Everywhere you look in the War Rooms, there are details that hint at what daily life must have been like here in wartime. Almost all staff worked in shifts, but were often required to stay at their desks well beyond their appointed hours. The officers had their own mess in what is now the museum shop, but would also eat at their clubs above ground. Other staff would also eat out at nearby cafes if possible but, after spring 1942, they could choose to eat at a canteen set up for them in a more distant part of the basement. Between shifts, staff could make their way home or make use of their accommodation — the lucky ones in private rooms on the basement level, the rest in dormitories a floor further down.

. . . .

The busy staff of the War Rooms were afforded their own post box for sending out personal correspondence. It was emptied four times a day. Staff walking down the main corridor could also check to see if they had received any personal mail.

POST
STAMPED LETTERS ONLY.
STAMPS ARE ON SALE IN THE MESS.
CLEARED AT 08,30 - 11,30 - 16,00 - 17,15.

▲ This wooden board on the wall of the main corridor was used to indicate either 'All Clear' or 'Warning', which meant that there was imminent danger overhead.

Lieutenant General Sir Leslie Hollis. c.1947

SECRECY

As Senior Assistant Secretary to the War Cabinet, Lieutenant General Sir Leslie Hollis was privy to all kinds of top secret information. Keeping it secret could be difficult and frustrating, as he explains in this extract from his memoirs:

'Outside the office, one was reluctant to talk about the war to anyone, however prominent or well-known. I remember travelling to my home in Sussex to see for a few hours my wife when she was ill. In the train there was one other civilian gentleman in the compartment. I was in uniform and the civilian started a conversation about the course of the war. His questions were very much to the point and I knew most of the answers, but in every case I pleaded complete ignorance. As I got off the train he gave me a withering look of contempt, as much as to say: "No wonder we are doing so badly when such flannelled fools are allowed to hold the King's Commission!"'

▶ In the interests of economy, lights were expected to be turned off whenever a room was not in use.

▼ In the summer of 1938 George Rance had been an Office of Works official, less than a year away from retirement. Over the following months he became integral to the development and everyday running of the War Rooms. To maintain secrecy, for example, all the furniture, maps and documents required to equip the site were addressed simply 'c/o Mr Rance, Office of Works, Whitehall'. During the war the Grenadier Guards protecting the War Rooms were nicknamed 'Rance's Guard'. After the war, Rance continued to watch over the site and he acted as an unofficial guide to interested parties. Here he is seen adjusting the weather indicator board – the only means by which staff could know what conditions to expect above ground.

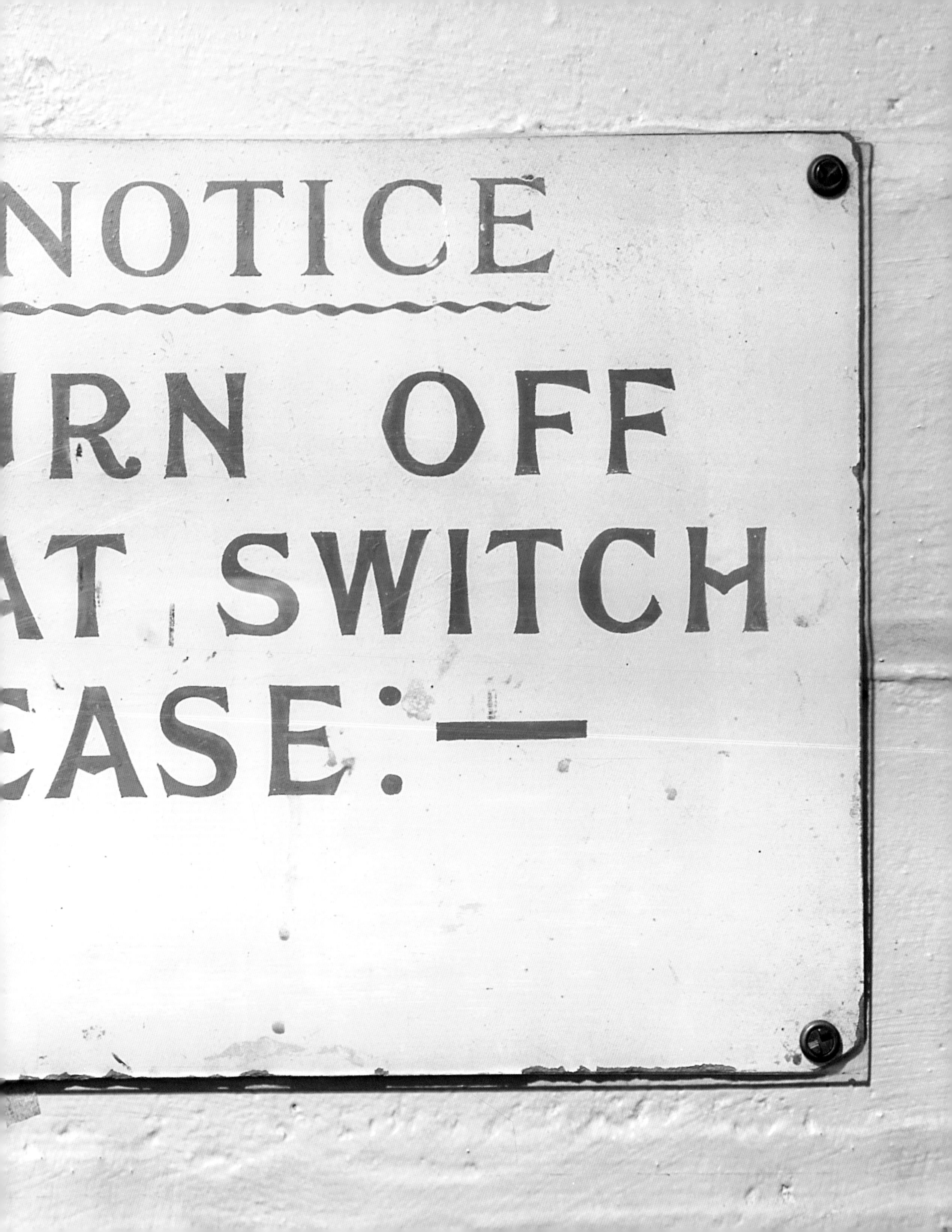

NOTICE

RN OFF

T SWITCH

ASE :—

◀ A group of men and women acted as cleaners of the War Rooms under the supervision of George Rance. The men covered the corridors and rooms in the main body of the War Rooms; the women worked in the other 'courtyard' rooms that were opened up elsewhere in the basement as the war progressed.

▶ The War Rooms had its own independent electrical supply system, incorporating specially armoured cables to withstand bomb damage. It also had a back-up system, which it appears was never used. The bulk of the system was situated and monitored in the Plant Room, with fuse boxes also scattered around the site.

▼ Churchill is credited with the invention of this label, which was used to mark the most urgent documents in circulation.

ACTION THIS DAY

G

H.M.O.W.
STAFF ONLY.

M.O.P.B. AND WORKS.
ROOM 24, SUB - GROUND FLOOR.
WHI.4300 - EXT.222

VENTILATION PLANT

PLANT ROOM Nº 7

KEEP SHUT

THIS DOCUMENT IS THE PROPERTY OF HIS BRITANNIC MAJESTY'S GOVERNMENT

The circulation of this paper has been strictly limited.

It is issued for the personal use of.............................

TOP
~~MOST~~ SECRET.   Copy No.............

MOST SECRET - TO BE BURNT BEFORE READING

J.P.(T)(42) 1 (FINAL)

9th May 1942

WAR CABINET

JOINT PLANNING TYPISTS

OPERATION "DESPERATE"

Report by the J.P. Typing Pool

In view of the recent changes in the Government policy
of distribution of coupons,* we have examined the situation,
and the following conclusions have been reached:-

(a) The limitation of supplies in the U.K. has resulted
in the following acute shortages -

(i) silk stockings;
(ii) chocolates;
(iii) cosmetics.

(b) The lack of these vital commodities is regarded as
extremely serious and may, in consequence, become
a source of extreme embarrassment. This must be
avoided at all costs.

(c) It is felt that immediate steps should be taken to
explore the possibilities of U.S. resources.

2.   In the light of the above, it is considered that the most
expedient method of implementing the proposal in (c) would be
the early despatch of a mission to the U.S.A; a Force Commander
has already been appointed, in anticipation of instructions.
Accordingly, we attach a draft directive* to the officer
concerned.

(Signed)   NAUSEA D. BAGWASH
LIZZI LIGHT-ffOOT
MAGGIE DEUCE
DEADLY NIGHTSHADE
JUNE WINTERBOTTHAM   (Mrs)

* As from May 31st - only 60 in 14 months!
β Annex

-1-

◀ In May 1942 – ahead of Churchill's second visit to Washington – some of the female staff in the War Rooms produced this light-hearted memorandum on the subject of Operation 'Desperate'. The mission it describes, which gives an insight into the dreary conditions endured by Britons during the war, is said to have been a complete success.

▶ To alleviate the health problems associated with working underground for prolonged periods of time, staff were made to strip to their underwear, put on a pair of protective goggles and stand in front of portable sun lamps like this one. Incidences of 'sunburn' were common, and one veteran recalls a 'silly girl' who forgot to put on the goggles and nearly went blind.

'We started with one minute each side and got up to probably ten minutes. I remember, being fair skinned, sometimes I would be as red as a beetroot.'

Leading Aircraftwoman Myra Murden on using the Sol Tan box

Operating Instructions

for

SOL-TAN

HIGH PRESSURE MERCURY
ARC ULTRA-VIOLET LAMPS

Nos. EM/96P, 97P, 98P, 99P, 365P,
415P, 415P/FM, 415/36P

THE CHIEFS OF STAFF CONFERENCE ROOM

In spring 1941 the expansion of the protective concrete slab above the War Rooms made another section of the basement available for use. By late July this large room was set aside as a reserve conference room for the Chiefs of Staff – the heads of the Army, Navy and Air Force. Most of the time the Chiefs would hold their meetings on the second floor of the building above the War Rooms, but they would often come down here during the V-weapon offensives in 1944 and 1945.

....

By the time of the V-weapon offensives, the Chiefs of Staff were Admiral of the Fleet Sir Andrew Cunningham, Air Chief Marshal Sir Charles Portal and General Sir Alan Brooke. The decisions that they made in this 'New Map Room' determined the movements of hundreds of thousands of military personnel across the globe.

'This is the powerhouse of war... these great men sitting there at the table. It was deeply moving.'

Alan Melville, a member of the Joint Planning Staff, on once attending a Chiefs of Staff meeting

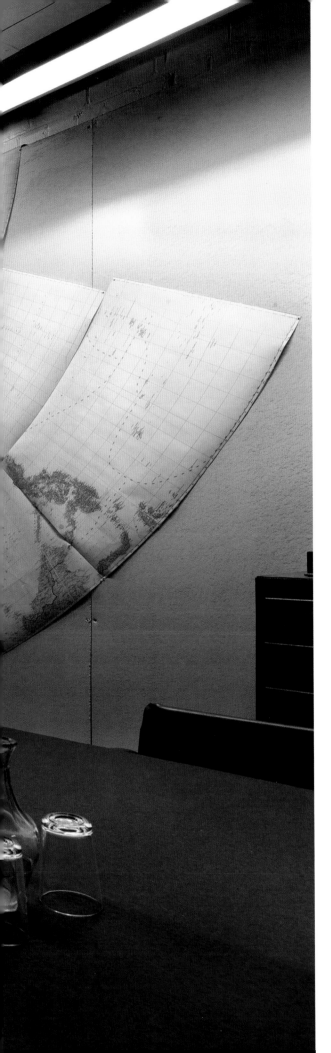

◀ The room has been restored as closely as possible to match photographs of the original layout taken in 1945. The maps on the walls, for example, were taken from the basement Map Room in the Admiralty. They are almost certainly the same ones used by Churchill in the first few months of the war when he was First Lord of the Admiralty.

▼ The chairs arranged around the table are almost exact replicas of those originally used. They are the same type as the ones seen in the War Cabinet Room.

The large map on the left-hand wall of the room sports a curious addition. If you trace a line due west from the far north-west tip of Scotland, you will come across this hand-drawn caricature of German leader Adolf Hitler. It is not known when this mocking piece of graffiti was added.

A photograph of the room taken in 1945 shows one small bar heater like this one, pointing towards the main meeting table. In such a large room, its task must have been a rather forlorn one.

The provision of a small ladder in the room points to the fact that support staff occasionally had to mark, alter or replace the maps on the walls.

THE MAP ROOM

The Map Room was the nerve centre of Britain's war effort. A week before the war began, a handpicked team of recently retired officers took up their positions at the bank of desks running along the centre of the room. Hours later, the next shift took their place, then the next and the next. It would be six years before the room was left empty again.

Every retreat and advance, every defeat and victory, was recorded in calm, unemotional and faithful detail within this inner sanctum. As one senior member of the War Rooms administrative staff put it: 'Daily truth belonged to the Map Room.'

Map Room officers at work, c.1945

During each shift, five men sat at the desks in the Map Room – one each from the Army, Navy and Air Force, another from the Ministry of Home Security, and a fifth man from each of the services in turn acting as the Duty Officer. It was their job to receive intelligence reports by telephone and on paper, sift through them and then pass on the details to a team of 'plotters' standing ready around the room. They then translated the information on to the maps mounted around the room. In this manner the Map Room acted as something like a scoreboard for the war.

Churchill was a great lover of maps and could often be found in the Map Room, especially when air raids forced the War Cabinet and Defence Committee to meet underground. He took great pleasure in showing the room off to special guests, including the King and Queen in 1942 and General Eisenhower, the Supreme Commander of the Allied Expeditionary Force, in 1944.

SUPPLYING THE MAPS

One of the key questions during the setting up of the Map Room was what maps it should contain. It was a difficult question to answer, as Brigadier George Davy explained in a letter to IWM in December 1982:

'War was in sight and [the Deputy Director of Operations at the War Office] asked me if I would stick up the relevant maps in the basement war room... Work space was limited among the concrete and he told me to go and look at it. I did, and when I went back and asked what maps he had in mind, he said: "Your guess is as good as mine." So I went ahead with the "Cockpit of Europe" at the larger scales, smaller for the fringes and tiny for the Far East where there was less certainty of trouble.'

◀ One of the most important duties of the Map Room staff was to help the Joint Planning staff prepare a daily briefing on the war situation for the Prime Minister, the Chiefs of Staff and the King. This 'CWR Bulletin' was made ready by eight o'clock every morning. As part of the distribution process, one copy was placed in this battered red leather dispatch box. This was then loaded onto a horse-drawn brougham carriage and driven the short distance to Buckingham Palace, where it was brought before the eyes of King George VI.

The telephones lined up along the desks were nicknamed the 'beauty chorus' by Map Room staff. The white phones were connected to the War Rooms of each of the three armed services; the green to intelligence sources; and the black to the outside world via a private telephone exchange. It was through these telephones that most information on the war situation was received.

Beside each phone in the Map Room is a switch that allowed incoming calls to be marked by a flashing light rather than a ringing bell. This was presumably a way to maintain calm during especially busy periods.

An enormous convoy map dominates one end of the Map Room. Viewed from a distance, it is still possible to see the cloud left behind by tens of thousands of tiny pinholes. Each time a pin was placed in the waters of the North Atlantic or Mediterranean it represented the position of a convoy running the gauntlet of German and Italian submarines to deliver vital supplies to Britain, its allies and its fighting forces. Sometimes it would denote progress, but all too often it would indicate that the ship had been sunk.

Baltic Sea

EACH PIN POINT
REPRESENTS A CONVOY
MOVEMENT. WITH CONVOYS

INDIAN OCEAN
CONVOY ESCORTS

Persian Gulf

Bombay

Colom

Algiers

Suez

Aden

Port Sudan

Massawa

Addu Atoll

Kilindini

Diego Suarez

Seychelles

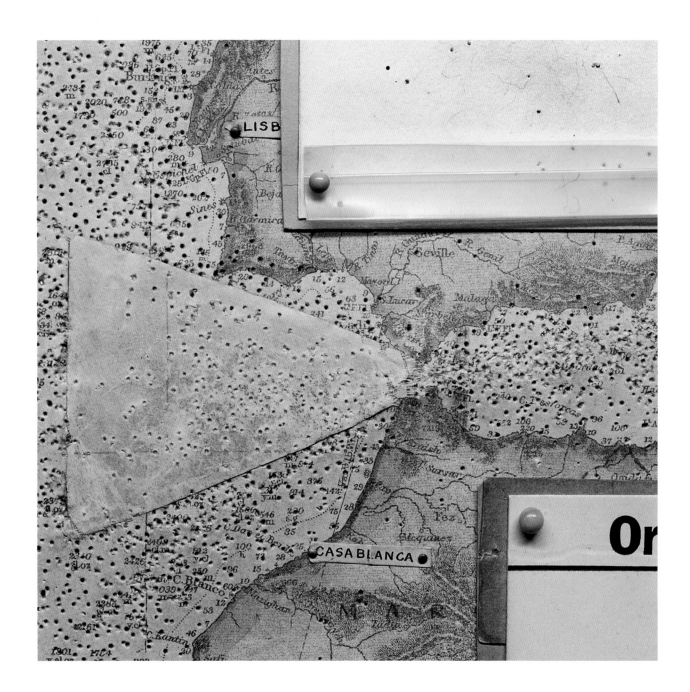

Viewed close-up, it is possible to make out other details on the convoy map, such as sections that became so worn with use that they were replaced; the addition of tags to mark important ports; and faint lines drawn, for example, to denote where Britain's home waters end and the West Atlantic begins.

These sugar cubes belonged to Wing Commander John Heagerty, one of the officers who manned the Map Room from 1939 through to 1945. Sugar was in short supply during the war, and Heagerty appears to have hidden his in an envelope at the back of one of his drawers, where it lay undisturbed until IWM conducted a thorough inventory of the War Rooms in the early 1980s. From the shape of one of the cubes, it looks as if the officer may have conducted his own rationing system, shaving off small amounts of sugar as and when he needed it.

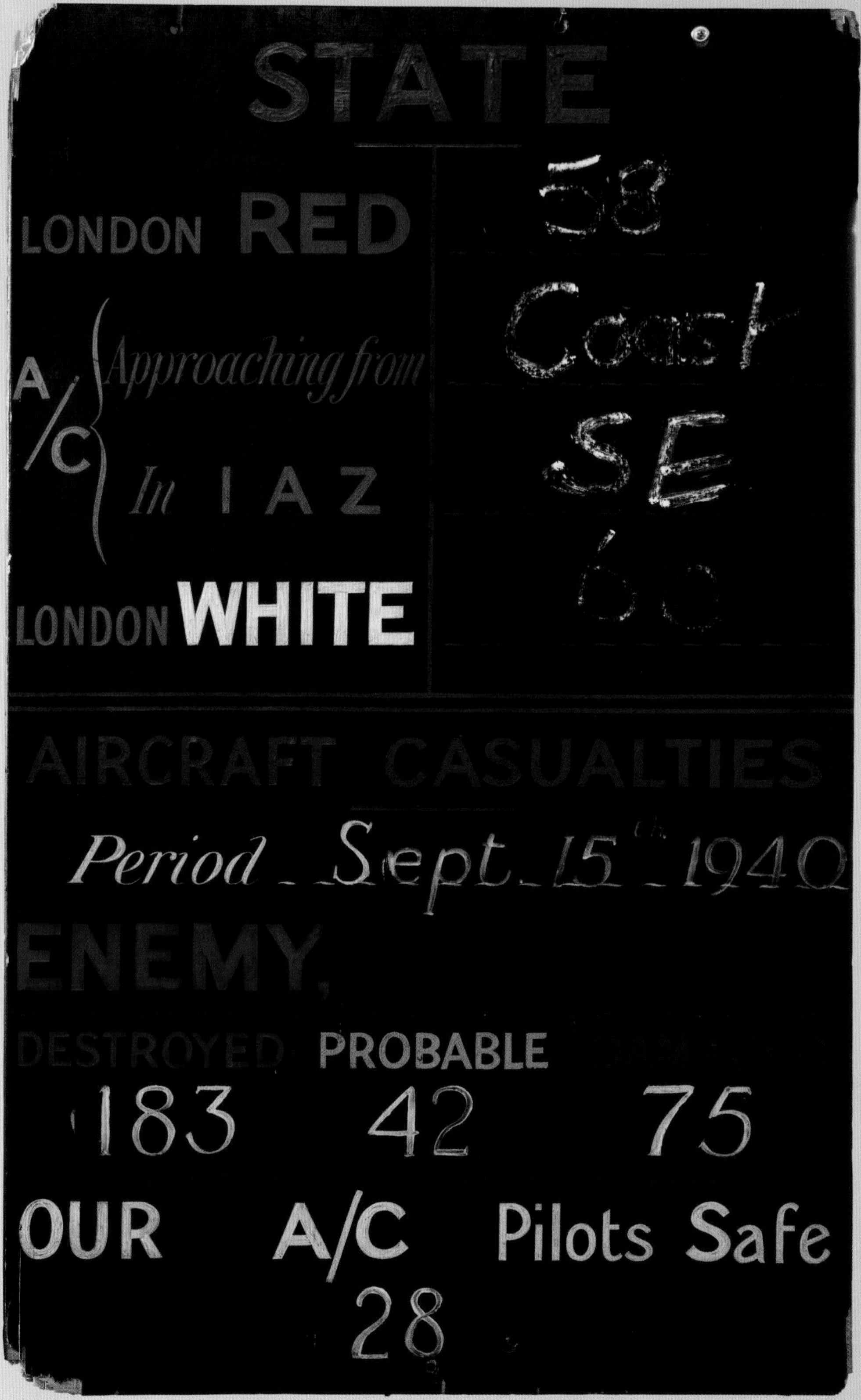

STATE

LONDON **RED**

A/C { *Approaching from* *In* I A Z

LONDON **WHITE**

58
Coast
SE
6c

AIRCRAFT CASUALTIES

Period Sept. 15th 1940

ENEMY,

DESTROYED   PROBABLE

183   42   75

OUR   A/C   Pilots Safe

28

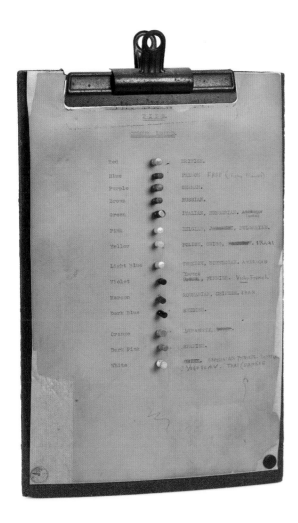

The Map Room in use, 1945

THE LURE OF THE MAP ROOM

As Deputy Secretary (Military) to the War Cabinet and Chief of Staff to Churchill, Major-General Hastings Ismay was one of the select few given access to the Map Room. Here he describes why he found it hard to resist going in:

'Whenever a big battle or critical movement was in progress, it was a temptation to find pretexts for going to the [Map Room] at all hours of the day and night, in order to get the latest information. The sensation was not unlike visiting a friend in hospital. One entered the room hoping for the best, but fearing the worst. "How is the Malta convoy going?" one would ask, trying not to appear unduly anxious. The nature of the answer could generally be guessed from the expression of the officer on duty... My visits often coincided with those of a sturdy figure in a siren suit, and I began to understand why my chief was always so embarrassingly up to date with every detail of the situation.'

▲ Every pin had a different significance according to its colour. This clipboard, which records the colour-coding used, makes it obvious just how global the Second World War became.

◀ During the Battle of Britain in the summer of 1940, Map Room staff would chalk up on this blackboard the number of enemy aircraft destroyed each day. Later one of the staff painted in these figures from 15 September to create a permanent record of the day that turned the battle decisively in Britain's favour.

▲ In the Map Room, as everywhere else in the War Rooms, the air would have been thick with cigarette smoke. One letter in the IWM archives describes how a colleague 'always smoked cigarettes' as he studied his maps. 'He used to pore over his contours making calculations and noting the results in countless numbers of extremely small figures ... his face always wreathed in smoke ... under the glare of a fluorescent tubular light.'

▶ This was the desk used by the Duty Officer – the Army, Navy or Air Force officer in charge of any given shift in the Map Room. As well as overseeing the work going on in the Map Room, the Duty Officer (alongside the Camp Commandant) was expected to take charge of the defence of the War Rooms if the site came under attack from enemy forces on the ground. Sitting close to the Duty Officer's desk was an ivory telephone, which connected the Map Room to the Prime Minister at 10 Downing Street.

▲ Miniature flags like these were prepared for every significant combatant nation. They came in little packs of 25.

◄ Only a small proportion of the maps were displayed in the Map Room at any one time. Most were filed away in drawers, either inside the room itself or in the corridor outside. Open up the drawers in the Map Room today and you will still find scores of original maps – covering everywhere from outer London to Mongolia, the Dodecanese Islands to the Yugoslavian railway system. Above one of the drawer units, but barely visible from the viewing area, there is a pulley system in place for the temporary mounting and display of maps.

Myra Murden

BEHIND THE SCENES OF THE MAP ROOM

The smooth operation of the Map Room depended on contributions from many members of staff behind the scenes. One of them was Leading Aircraftwoman Myra Murden, who here explains what her role was and how she came to do it:

'There were these tiny little cubby-hole places and I remember sitting and doing short-hand and typing there... One night I was just sitting there and waiting and I was drawing a rose, because I loved drawing. And this civilian went by and he said "Right, you can work for us tomorrow." And with that I went through another trap door into a lower room... to work for these three draftsmen... They used to do all these huge maps that went down to the Cabinet Room every day...

'I did the labels and I suppose the grotty jobs, but that didn't worry me... And these three men, they did all the important secret work on the maps.

'There was one huge map in the morning... they would put little crosses and things across the Atlantic where U-boats or submarines or ships had been sunk. And it was my job to draw a little submarine and put a little English flag on, or swastika, or a ship on its side...'

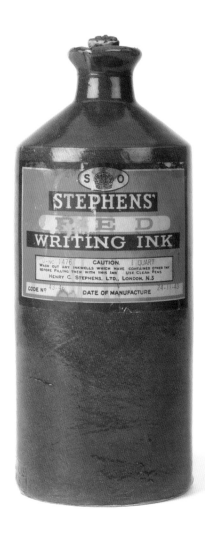

▲ When the Map Room officers and clerks arrived at their desks a week before the war began, they found eight boxes waiting for them. Inside them was a 'Massive Reserve Stationery Kit', which was supposed to include everything they would need – from ink bottles like these to envelopes and paperclips. On closer examination, they discovered that it did not contain any coloured card, so this was the one thing they had to do without in the first few days of the war.

This cigarette lighter was rigged up by an electrician during the war. Pressing the button on the right heated a wire filament from which Map Room officers could light their cigarettes. It is thought the device was used to limit the fire hazard presented by naked flames from ordinary cigarette lighters and matches.

S E C R E T   COPY NO. ____

CABINET WAR ROOM RECORD NO. 2074

For the 24 hours ending 0700, 8th May, 1945

1.   In accordance with an agreement signed on 7th May, all
German forces in Europe surrendered unconditionally to the
Allies, the "cease-fire" to come into force with effect
from 0001 hours 9th May.

MILITARY

2.   Western Europe.   The Third U.S. Army has continued to
advance along the DANUBE valley east of LINZ and further north
is sweeping through Western Czechoslovakia on a very wide front.
It is confirmed that PILSEN was captured by U.S. Armoured forces
on the 6th.
      The Second British Army has reached the line of the KIEL
Canal and further west is approaching CUXHAVEN.
      The First Canadian Army has cleared the country between
the WESER and the EMS and occupied EMDEN.

3.   Italy.   U.S. forces are now stationed alongside New Zealand
and British troops in TRIESTE, where the situation remains quiet.

4.   Russian Front.   The Russians have reached the River ELBE to
the north and S.E. of MAGDEBURG.   They have captured BRESLAU and
made further progress west and S.W. of MORAVSKA OSTRAVA.

AIR

5.   Western Front.   Yesterday,   Allied aircraft dropped 1545 tons
of food supplies in HOLLAND.
      408 fighters (2 missing) provided support for the advance
into CZECHOSLOVAKIA: 2 enemy aircraft were destroyed in combat.

6.   French Indo-China.   On the 4th, 47 Liberators dropped 91 tons
on the naval dockyard and arsenal at SAIGON.   Enemy casualties in
combat 2:3:0.

NAVAL

7.   Home Waters.   A naval party which has arrived at EMDEN has found
the port apparently in good order.   Twenty-five minor warships
are present but no U-boats.

8.   Pacific.   The British Pacific Fleet has resumed operations
against the SAKISHIMA Islands.   Battleships carried out a bombardment
and carrier-borne aircraft attacked airfields.   In an attack on
H.M. carriers by Japanese aircraft, FORMIDABLE was slightly
damaged: 8 aircraft were shot down.

9.   Enemy Attack on Shipping.

AVONDALE PARK (2878)   ) sunk by U-boat in coastal convoy
SNELAND ISLAND(1791) Norwegian) off the Firth of Forth yesterday.

Cabinet War Room

8th May, 1945

▲ A member of staff highlighted the 'V' on the Map Room clock in red, echoing the 'V' sign used by Winston Churchill to signify Victory.

◄ The Map Room officers helped to produce a daily report which was circulated to the King, Prime Minister, Chiefs of Staff and other officers on every morning of the war. This extract from the report, covering 'the 24 hours ending 0700, 8th May, 1945', shows how victory in Europe was accorded just one short bullet point before the rest of the business of the day followed.

PACIFIC

NEW GUINEA.
FORCE HD. QRS. TPS.
- 11. AUST. DIV.
- NON DIVISIONAL.
- 6. AUST.

NEW BRITAIN
- NON DIVISIONAL.
- 135. US.
- A.I.F.
- NON DIVISIONAL.
- 172. US. CAV.

I US. MARINE AMPHIBIOUS CORPS.

- 19. US.
- 8. N.Z.

S.P. ISLANDS.

NEW HEBRIDES.	SAMOAN.
GILBERTS.	CANTON.
ELLICE.	PENRHEN.
PALMYRA.	CHRISTMAS.
FANNING.	AITUKAKI.

- 5. AUST. DIV.
- 4. AUST.
- 8. AUST.

ADV. 6 (U.S.) ARMY.
- I. US. INF.
- 62. US. INF.
- 40. US. INF.
- 32. (U.S.) DIV.
- 126. REGT.
- 1. REGT.
- 128. REGT.
- 33. US. DIV.
- 123. US.
- 130. US.
- 31. US. DIV.
- 155. US. INF.
- 154. US. INF.
- 24. (US.) DIV.
- 19. US. INF.
- 21. US. INF.
- 3. HUS. INF.

1 US. CORPS.
- 41. US. DIV.
- 163. US. INF.
- 4. US.

- 108. US. INF.
- 160. US.
- 185. US. INF.

ADMIRALTY ISLANDS.
- I. US. C. A. V. BN.
- 2. US. C. A. V. BN.
- 1. US. CAV.
- 166. US.
- NON DIVISIONAL.
- 1. (US.) CAV.
- 2. US. CAV.

EMIRAU ISLAND
- 147. US. INF.
- 16. US. INF.

DUTCH NEW GUINEA.
- HD. QRS. 4 AUST. DIV.

S.W.P. ISLANDS.
- U.S. DETMTS.
- KIRIWINA.
- WOODLARK.

SOLOMONS.
XIV US. CORPS.
- NON DIVISIONAL.
- TWO... 132. US. INF.
- 164. US. INF.
- 182. US. INF.
- 3. US. M.
- 9. US. M.
- 21. US. M.
- 37. US. DIV.
- 135. US. INF.
- 145. (US.) INF.
- 148. US. INF.
- 93. US. DIV.
- 25. US. INF.
- 368. US. INF.
- 25. US. INF.
- 3. N.Z. DIV.
- 8. 14. N.Z.

- 7. US. DIV.
- 17. US. INF.
- 32. US. INF.
- 90. US. INF.
- 6. US. DIV.
- SOCIETY.
- NEW CALEDONIA.
- BR. + US. DETMTS.
- TONGA.
- FIJI
- BRIT. DETMTS.
- NORFOLK.
- 4. US.
- 32. US.
- 184. US.
- 27. US. DIV.
- 105. US. INF.
- 165. US. INF.

HAWAII
- NON DIVISIONAL.
- 185.
- 159.
- 4. US. MARINE DIV.
- 30.
- 24.
- 25.
- NON DIVISIONAL.
- 4.

ALASKA + ALEU...
MARSHAL...

▲ The date displayed in the Map Room is the day in 1945 that the War Rooms were used for the last time. Japan had surrendered just hours earlier. The war was over.

◀ The Map Room has been preserved to look almost exactly as it did at the end of the war. Many of the maps, charts and lists on the walls therefore reflect Allied preoccupations in the final days of the conflict – such as this table showing Allied air strength in the South-West and South Pacific at the end of April 1945.

PRESERVING CHURCHILL'S WAR ROOMS

Filed away in the archives of IWM is a small folder containing correspondence between the museum and the government in the months after August 1945. Reading the various letters, memos and notes it is clear that while everyone was quick to recognise the historical value of the War Rooms, there was no clear plan for what should happen to them after the war. There was talk of recreating the Map Room as an exhibit within the museum, and suggestions were made on both sides about specific objects that the museum should acquire – Churchill's chair from the Cabinet Room perhaps and the Convoy Map with its hundreds of thousands of pin holes – but in the end no agreement could be reached.

The only significant step taken by IWM during this period was an arrangement to send a photographer to take a visual record of the site. The images that he captured – some time in either August or September 1945 – show the War Rooms being well looked after. George Rance, the Office of Works employee responsible for the maintenance of the site during the war, can still be seen in attendance, as can several of the Royal Marine orderlies. And all the rooms, though unoccupied by staff, are pictured still ready for use – from the Churchills' dining room to the Officers' Mess.

In the year after the photographs were taken, large sections of the site were stripped out and returned to general government use. Only a handful of rooms were left untouched – the Map Room and its annexe, the Transatlantic Telephone Room, the Cabinet Room and Churchill's bedroom. One motivating factor for the temporary preservation of these rooms was the level of interest shown in them by the public. In September 1946 Lawrence Burgis, one of the Cabinet Office officials who had helped to set up the War Rooms, wrote:

> I have been astonished at the amount of interest shown in the CWR by the outside public and such like and have always given them every facility to visit the place... And of course Mr Rance is a marvellous guide.

It appears then that groups of visitors were already being given unofficial tours of the rooms at this very early stage. More remarkably still, the preserved rooms still contained a great many top secret documents. It was only thought wise to remove these in November 1947.

The level of public interest grew so great that it was decided to put the preservation of the rooms on a more official basis. This decision was announced in Parliament early in 1948, and a press conference was held in the War Rooms themselves on 17 March. Photographs of this occasion can be found in the IWM archive, showing Ismay and Rance making a presentation to journalists and then

Ismay and Rance show journalists the Map Room, March 1948

leading them on a tour of the rooms. It was a tour that Rance would continue to lead for other groups until 1950, when ill-health forced him to step down at the age of 76. A retired Royal Marine took his place.

During the 1950s and 1960s – as the Cold War reached its height – members of the public visiting the War Rooms would have been astonished to discover that secret work was still being carried out just yards away from where they were standing. Rooms 62, 62A and 62B, for example, were adapted for use by the Chiefs

of Staff to serve as a conference room, teleprinter room and cypher room, and the whole complex was earmarked to act as 'Quarters for the central Government in the event of an emergency'. Indeed, documents in the IWM archive suggest that a command centre was re-established in the War Rooms during the Suez Crisis of 1956. Chief among them is a letter (shown right) received in November 1956 by former Map Room officer Wing Commander John Heagerty. It came from a former colleague, Air Marshal William Dickson, who wrote:

RECEIVED
23 NOV 1956
Ansd.

MINISTRY OF DEFENCE,
STOREY'S GATE,
S.W.1.

22nd November, 1956.

Dear John,

Many thanks for your letter of 5th November, 1956, which I should have answered before but overlooked in the rush. I am very sorry indeed to have to reply that I cannot come to the C.W.R. dinner next Tuesday. My excuse is a good one because that night I am dining with the Queen and the Army Council!

Please remember me to all my old friends. You may like to tell them that we opened up the C.W.R. for our little war in the Middle East. It was humming with activity all down the corridor and the old mess at the end of the corridor was revived and the famous green tin cupboard in the corner restocked with drink. They even had one of the old Marines back again (I forget his name). We did not touch your old map room, which is still there as a museum, but made another one out of one of the rooms nearer the mess. All this brought 1939/45 back vividly to memory. We even issued the daily C.W.R. Summary to Ministers on the famous paper.

Best wishes for a very happy reunion.

Yours ever,

Diki.

P.S.   I am fully fit again, thank you.

Wing Commander J. Heagerty,
    36, Walpole Street,
        Chelsea,
            London, S.W.3.

We opened up the CWR for our little war in the Middle East. It was humming with activity all down the corridor and the old mess at the end of the corridor was revived and the famous green tin cupboard in the corner restocked with drink... We did not touch your old map room, which is still there as a museum, but made another one out of the rooms nearer the mess. All of this brought 1939-45 back vividly to memory. We even issued the daily CWR Summary to Ministers on the famous paper.

Another document in the Ministry of Defence archives reveals that in 1961 the Chiefs of Staff wanted to reclaim at least part of the area being shown to visitors. The idea was 'to establish a War Room manned permanently on a skeleton basis', but it does not seem to have come to fruition.

By the 1970s almost 5,000 visitors were touring the rooms every year. There was no set route for this tour; visitors were simply escorted into each room in turn and allowed to look around as the mood took them. In 1974 one member of IWM staff noted with a certain amount of disapproval: 'It is quite normal for visitors to bounce up and down on the Prime Minister's bed, to sit in his chair and look into the drawers of his desk.'

Concerns were also growing about the state of the rooms themselves, where the dry and dusty conditions were taking their toll on less durable items such as soft furnishings and documents. The government eventually decided to spend £7,000 on conservation work, but also began looking for ways to recoup these costs and make the site more self-sustaining. One idea was to open up the War Rooms to more visitors and to charge them a fee for entry. There were certainly plenty of people keen to see the site – every year the Cabinet Office received applications from 30,000 to 40,000 potential visitors, but had to turn the vast majority away.

In 1974, IWM was asked to take on the project. On one level it was an extremely attractive prospect, especially to the museum's then Director-General Dr Noble Frankland, who had spent several years in the War Rooms after the war working on an official history of Bomber Command. Eventually, however, the museum's trustees decided to turn down the opportunity, citing the financial commitments it

already had to its new branch at Duxford, which opened in 1976, and HMS *Belfast* in 1978.

The question was posed again in 1981 – this time with the personal backing of Prime Minister Margaret Thatcher. Negotiations were held with the National Trust and Madame Tussauds, but IWM remained the government's preferred choice. In January 1982 the museum duly agreed to take over the management of the site, on the condition that the Department of the Environment pay for the setting-up costs. The scene was now set for two years of extraordinary work, preserving the key rooms that had been open to the public since the end of the war, and restoring over a dozen more to their wartime appearance.

To begin with the plan was to stick to the tried and tested procedure of escorting small groups of visitors in and out of the rooms, so preserving the original structure and layout of the site. Eventually, however, it was decided to create a one-way route for visitors to circulate around unescorted, and to glaze off the rooms so that they could be viewed without being entered. Before any structural work could take place, the contents of the rooms had to be catalogued and removed for conservation and storage elsewhere. Copies of this original inventory are still held by IWM. Room by room, object by object, some 7,000 items were numbered, described and measured, and their locations recorded in painstaking detail. Take, for example, object number E69B-3-3 in the War Cabinet Room. It is a paper knife with sheath and rubber, measuring 19cm in length, positioned 10cm from the front edge of the table and 145cm from the edge of the table closest to 'Wall I'. It was there when IWM took over the site in 1982, and it was back in the exact same position when restoration work on the rooms was complete.

Much of the structural work on the site involved creating openings in the existing fabric of the building to allow visitors to see into the rooms and to provide a straightforward one-way route to move around the building. Between Room 62B and the Map Room Annexe this involved drilling a passageway through a chamber that had been filled with concrete to strengthen the site during the war. The job was expected to take about three weeks to complete, but such was the quality of the concrete that it took three months.

There were other challenges too: the adaptation of the wartime ventilation trunking to allow for two separate ventilation systems (one for the public areas, one to create a stringently controlled atmosphere to protect the contents of the sealed rooms); the rewiring of the site while retaining all of the original lamps and fittings; and the careful cleaning of the rooms to restore them to their wartime appearance.

While all of this work was going on, IWM historians Peter Simkins, Mike Houlihan and Jon Wenzel were hard at work piecing together the story of the War Rooms – no easy task given that the site was constructed, developed and operated in such secrecy. They were ably assisted by Nigel de Lee, who was then a teacher at the Royal Military Academy, Sandhurst. It was his role to delve deeply into the government's archives to uncover the key decisions and correspondence that underpinned every aspect of the site's history.

Simkins, Houlihan and Wenzel built on de Lee's factual foundations by trawling through the papers, diaries and autobiographies of the main players in the War Rooms story, including Churchill, Ismay, Hollis, Alanbrooke and Bridges – all of whom had died before the restoration process began. They conducted interviews with the few surviving senior staff such as Sir John Colville and Sir John Winnifrith (establishment officer of the War Cabinet Office), and consulted the far greater number of surviving junior officers, secretaries and personal assistants, most of whom had of course been much younger during their wartime service.

All of this research helped the historians establish the facts of how the War Rooms were used at different points during the war. It was a messy story, with many of the rooms being divided and sub-divided and their uses changing as Britain's wartime priorities evolved. It was therefore decided to restore the rooms to look as they would have done during their 'period of maximum use', which by and large boiled down to the months between the end of the Battle of France in summer 1940 and the end of the Blitz in spring 1941.

It fell to Jon Wenzel, who was to become the first curator of the War Rooms, to source all the furniture, fixtures and fittings required to make the reconstruction of the rooms as accurate as possible. Fortunately, all of the furniture used in the site turned out to have been standardised (with the exception of the Prime Minister's room), and Wenzel was able to source much of it by submitting regular 'shopping lists' to the furniture clearing warehouse run by the government's Property Services Agency. He was also given access to different government departments to look for typewriters, chairs and wicker baskets that had managed to remain part of civil service life since the 1940s.

The decision was also made to include Tussaud-like waxworks to give a better impression of the rooms in use. The creation of these figures was subject to a great deal of care and attention. Volunteers were brought in to assume particular positions and then casts were made from which the mannequins were constructed. Their poses were chosen to add a sense of movement to the rooms. One officer is shown searching for something in a cupboard, but look more closely and you can see that the phone on his desk is off the hook – someone on the other end of the line is clearly waiting for him to find the right document. Finally came the display panels, audio-guides and guidebooks that would help visitors gain a full understanding not only of what the War Rooms were for, but also what it was like to work there. Here the input of former War Rooms staff was especially invaluable, with their insights, impressions and anecdotes bringing the site to life for generations of visitors.

On 4 April 1984 many of those staff members were in attendance – alongside members of Churchill's family – when the War Rooms were formally opened to the public by Prime Minister Margaret Thatcher. Two days later at 10.00am the first paying visitor, Mrs C Hockenhull, was welcomed by Jon Wenzel and asked to sign the Cabinet War Rooms visitors' book.

Over the next few years hundreds of thousands of visitors flocked to the site, more than vindicating the decision to open it up to the public. Nonetheless, only a third of the original basement site was accessible for viewing – measuring little more than 1,000 square metres. During wartime many more rooms had been in use, which had since been stripped out and returned to general government use. Some became little more than casual dumping grounds for the government offices above, and

Margaret Thatcher is given a tour of the site after formally opening the War Rooms, 4 April 1984

one room was even converted to a gym. In 1993 there came a new director for the War Rooms in the shape of Phil Reed, who began pressing for these other sections of the basement to be made available to IWM. By 2001, he had successfully secured access to an additional area of over 2,000 square metres, and work began to put it to use.

The first section to be opened up in 2003 included the so-called Churchill Suite, containing the rooms originally set aside for the Prime Minister and his family and entourage. The photographs taken of the site back in

1945 proved to be a vital resource as museum staff set about locating the fixtures, fittings and furniture necessary for the restoration. The search took them through old government offices and second-hand shops, and even to the house at Windsor Great Park once occupied by Queen Elizabeth, the Queen Mother, where a plate-warmer was found to match the one used in the Churchills' kitchen.

Other sections of the basement were converted into an education facility, conference centre and cafe for the site, but the largest space was set aside to become

The Churchill Museum, which opened in 2005

the Churchill Museum – designed to tell the story of the wartime Prime Minister's remarkable 90-year life. Opened in 2005, 60 years after the end of the war and 40 years after Churchill's death, the museum is a superb modern counterpart to the preserved wartime rooms. Its centrepiece is the Churchill Lifeline – a 15-metre-long, electronic table that acts as an interactive timeline of Sir Winston's life. Visitors can use a touch strip along the side of the table to scroll through Churchill's life year by year and even day by day, and they can also pull up thousands of documents, images, animations and films to bring different parts of his story to life.

The addition of the Churchill Museum has breathed new life into the War Rooms, with visitor numbers climbing from around 300,000 in 2005 to a new high of almost 500,000 in 2015. Over 70 years after the Second World War, the remarkable story of Churchill and his War Rooms – so carefully preserved and restored by IWM – continues to captivate and enthral.

About the Author

Jonathan Asbury is the author of the official Churchill War Rooms guidebook, as well as guidebooks for HMS *Belfast*, IWM London, IWM North and IWM Duxford. He is a graduate of Churchill College, Cambridge – founded in honour of the wartime Prime Minister – and has enjoyed a life-long fascination with the way that the Second World War was won.

Acknowledgements

I had just finished writing a new visitor's guidebook for Churchill War Rooms when I was asked to provide the text for this more in-depth volume. Inevitably that new guidebook leant heavily on its predecessors, especially the first and most comprehensive of them (known as 'the bible' by present-day IWM staff). Produced in readiness for the opening of the War Rooms to the public in 1984, its author was Peter Simkins, one of IWM's in-house historians, who played a major role in the preservation and restoration of the site.

Simkins in turn relied on an unpublished history of the War Rooms, prepared by Nigel de Lee from the Royal Military Academy, Sandhurst. This history, which survives as a manuscript in the IWM archives, is an invaluable resource, based on a meticulous examination of government records and other primary source material. It is on de Lee's scholarly work that all subsequent histories of the War Rooms rely.

IWM also used de Lee's work as the factual foundation for the physical restoration of the site – determining as far as possible the precise function of each room, who worked where, and how the use of the basement evolved during the war. But the IWM team needed more. They needed to know the telling details: how particular rooms were set out, what ad-hoc arrangements were made that were never recorded in official government documents and, most importantly, what it felt like to be here on a day-to-day basis. They needed to talk to the people who knew the War Rooms best – the men and women who worked, ate and slept here as bombs rained down on the streets above.

Two other IWM historians, Mike Houlihan and Jon Wenzel, worked alongside Simkins and de Lee to track down, correspond with and talk to a wide range of War Rooms veterans, drawing out the kind of insights and stories that have since brought the site back to life. As a result of this research, IWM now has an extraordinary archive of personal papers and audio interviews, which has proved to be a crucial resource in putting together this book. (It was especially useful, for example, to see a donated copy of the Standing Instructions for the War Rooms – a document communicating all the mundane details that staff needed to know.)

Some of the IWM team's original notes and memos have also survived, stored in filing cabinets behind the scenes at the War Rooms. When I first began research on this book, Phil Reed, the outgoing Director of Churchill War Rooms, kindly allowed me access to these files, which include the meticulous inventory taken when IWM took over the site in the early 1980s, and other fascinating nuggets such as a BBC engineer's description of how Churchill's radio broadcasts from the basement were arranged.

Phil Reed himself proved to be an outstanding source of information and inspiration, regaling me with anecdotes from his thirteen years in charge of the site and treating me to a personal tour of some of the key rooms – the excitement of which I have tried to capture in this book. His love for the underground complex was evident and infectious, and his knowledge of the site is unsurpassed. Future historians would do well to capture more of his expertise on paper or as part of IWM's own audio archive.

Of course, not all of our understanding of the War Rooms comes from IWM's archives. First-hand insight into the site's inner workings began to emerge in the decades after the war – in the memoirs and diaries of key players such as General Lord Ismay, General Sir Leslie Hollis, Field Marshal Lord Alanbrooke, John Colville, Elizabeth Nel, Joan Bright Astley and, of course, Churchill himself. I also owe a profound debt to two excellent works of history: *Churchill's Bunker*, in which Professor Richard Holmes weaves together a masterly account of life in the secret headquarters; and Roy Jenkins' superb biography of Churchill, which I found an immensely valuable guide to the broader context of the war.

Working on this book has been a privilege. I would like to thank Liz Bowers and David Fenton of IWM for asking me to get involved, former director of Churchill War Rooms Phil Reed for his generosity and support, exhibitions manager Lucy Tindle for helping with the photo shoots, Ian Kikuchi and Lucy Tindle again for casting their expert eyes over the text, Andrew Tunnard for his superb photography and readiness to pitch in, Stephen Long for working his design alchemy on a trickily constructed manuscript, and Madeleine James and the rest of the publishing team at IWM for guiding me so patiently along the way.

I would also like to thank my mum and dad for their continuing love and support, George, Herbie, Iris, Connie and Martha for sparing me a few hours here and there to get on with writing this book, and Kathryn whose steadfast love, understanding and friendship has made it possible for me to pursue what the Chinese might call an 'interesting' career.

Sources

Bibliography

Alanbrooke, Field Marshal Lord (ed. Alex Danchev and Daniel Todman), *War Diaries 1939-45* (1992)
© The Estate of Field Marshal Alan Francis Brooke, 1st Viscount Alanbrooke

Astley, Joan Bright, *The Inner Circle. A View of the War at the Top* (1971)
© The Estate of Joan Bright Astley

Churchill, Winston, *The Complete Speeches Volume VI* (1974)
Reproduced with permission of Curtis Brown, London, on behalf of The Estate of Winston S. Churchill. © The Estate of Winston S. Churchill

Churchill, Winston, *The Second World War* (1948-53)
Reproduced with permission of Curtis Brown, London, on behalf of The Estate of Winston S. Churchill. © The Estate of Winston S. Churchill

Colville, John, *The Fringes of Power: Downing Street Diaries 1939-55* (1985)
© The Estate of Sir John Colville

de Lee, Nigel, *History of the Cabinet War Rooms 1939-45* (unpublished manuscript c.1983)

Finch, Cressida, *A Short History of the Cabinet War Rooms 1945-84*, (article for *Despatches: The Magazine of the Friends of IWM*, summer 2009)

Gilbert, Martin, *Winston S. Churchill, Vol. 6, Finest Hour 1939-41* (1983)
– *Winston S. Churchill, Vol.7, Road to Victory 1941-45* (1986)

Hickman, Tom, *Churchill's Bodyguard* (2008)

Hollis, General Sir Leslie, *One Marine's Tale* (1956)
© The Estate of General Sir Leslie Hollis

Holmes, Richard, *Churchill's Bunker. The Secret Headquarters at the Heart of Britain's Victory* (2009)

Ismay, General Lord, *Memoirs* (1960)
© The Estate of General Lord Hastings Ismay, 1st Baron Ismay

Jenkins, Roy, *Churchill* (2002)

Leasor, James, *War at the Top* (1959)

Moody, Joanna, *From Churchill's War Rooms. Letters of a Secretary 1943-45* (2007)

Nel, Elizabeth, *Winston Churchill by his Private Secretary* (2007 ed.)

Nicolson, Harold, *Letters and Diaries, 1939-45* (1966)
© The Estate of Sir Harold Nicolson

Sandys, Celia, *Churchill* (2013 ed.)

Simkins, Peter, *Cabinet War Rooms* (1983)

Singer, Barry, *Churchill Style* (2012)

Soames, Mary, *A Daughter's Tale* (2012)
© The Estate of Mary Soames

Soames, Mary (ed), *Speaking for Themselves* (1999)
Clementine Spencer-Churchill quotations reproduced with permission of Churchill Archives Centre, Churchill College.

Thompson, Walter H, *I Was Churchill's Shadow* (1951)
© The Estate of Walter H Thompson

IWM Audio Archive

3168, Air Vice Marshal Sir William Dickson

3444, Wendy Maxwell (née Wallace)
© James Holland

6191, Lieutenant-General Sir Ian Jacob

6356, Sir John Winnifrith

6380, Sir John Colville

6858, Stephen Geis © Stephen M Geis

9539, Frank Higgins

12441, Joint Planning officer Alan Melville

15119, Elizabeth Nel (née Layton)

18162, Joint Planning officer David Lee

18163, Ilene Adams (née Hutchinson)
© Ilene Hutchinson

19836, Joan Bright-Astley

23845, Leading Aircraftwoman Myra Collyer (née Murden)

31053, Aircraftswoman Rachel Foster

33037, Patrick Kinna

Private papers lodged with IWM

Lieutenant Colonel E N Buxton

18163 Ilene Adams (nee Hutchinson)

Documents.2773 General Sir Leslie Hollis

Documents.2995 Wing Commander John Heagerty

There are also files of miscellaneous papers relating to the War Rooms, including items such as the Standing Instructions for staff.

Filed correspondence between IWM and CWR staff

Brigadier Davy

Captain Ray Edghill
© The Estate of Captain Ray Edghill

Mrs Margaret d'Arcy

Mr H J Gregory

There are also copies of the inventory taken when IWM took over the site in the early 1980s, as well as countless other useful memos and reports.

Quotations by Winston Churchill reproduced with permission of Curtis Brown, London, on behalf of The Estate of Winston S. Churchill. © The Estate of Winston S. Churchill.

Image List

All images © IWM unless otherwise stated. Every effort has been made to contact all copyright holders. The publishers will be glad to make good in future editions any error or omissions brought to their attention.

Introduction
IWM (MH 26392)

Chapter 1
MH 27616; HU 48566; COL 30; © Shutterstock.com; MH 520; IWM 18163; Documents.2995; IWM_SITE_CWR_186; MH 534; IWM_SITE_CWR_188; IWM_SITE_CWR_196; CWR_1824; IWM 3444; IWM_SITE_CWR_000459; Documents_017438_A_1; IWM_SITE_CWR_000617; IWM_SITE_CWR_000619; IWM_SITE_CWR_000618; IWM_SITE_CWR_000620; IWM_SITE_CWR_000616; IWM_SITE_CWR_000110; IWM_SITE_CWR_000615; IWM_SITE_CWR_000621; IWM_SITE_CWR_000660; IWM_SITE_CWR_000661; IWM_SITE_CWR_000663; IWM_SITE_CWR_000472; CWR_000723_1; IWM_SITE_CWR_000593; A_030046_Ismay; IWM_SITE_CWR_000588; MH_000524; IWM_SITE_CWR_000587; IWM_SITE_CWR_000589; IWM_SITE_CWR_000591; IWM_SITE_CWR_000500; IWM_SITE_CWR_000062; IWM_SITE_CWR_000060; IWM_SITE_CWR_000592

Chapter 2
H_3978; HU_45910; HU_45913; IWM_SITE_CWR_000464; IWM_SITE_CWR_000468; IWM_SITE_CWR_000103; IWM 15119; IWM_SITE_CWR_000461; MH_000533; IWM_SITE_CWR_000623; IWM_SITE_CWR_000604; IWM_SITE_CWR_000603; IWM_SITE_CWR_000605; IWM_SITE_CWR_000668; IWM_SITE_CWR_000607; IWM_SITE_CWR_000583; IWM_SITE_CWR_000586; IWM_SITE_CWR_000584; IWM_SITE_CWR_000585; FEQ_000864; NYF_019390; IWM_SITE_CWR_000496; IWM_SITE_CWR_000497; IWM_SITE_CWR_000652; IWM_SITE_CWR_000449; IWM_SITE_CWR_000649; IWM_SITE_CWR_000654; IWM_SITE_CWR_000653; CWR_001991; IWM_SITE_CWR_000655; IWM_SITE_CWR_000580 & CWR_002059; CWR_002056; IWM_SITE_CWR_000509; IWM_SITE_CWR_000508; IWM_SITE_CWR_000675; IWM_SITE_CWR_000669; IWM_SITE_CWR_000448; MH_000538; IWM_SITE_CWR_000637; IWM_SITE_CWR_000499; IWM_SITE_CWR_000632; IWM_SITE_CWR_000633; IWM_SITE_CWR_000631; IWM_SITE_CWR_000636;

Chapter 3
E_18980; A_18749; IWM_SITE_CWR_000639; IWM_SITE_CWR_000638; H_16478; IWM_SITE_CWR_000566; HU_043546; IWM_SITE_CWR_000561; IWM_SITE_CWR_000563; IWM_SITE_CWR_000564; IWM_SITE_CWR_000642; IWM_SITE_CWR_000643; IWM_SITE_CWR_000645; IWM_SITE_CWR_000647; IWM_SITE_CWR_000484; IWM_SITE_CWR_000648; IWM_SITE_CWR_000640; H_3512; IWM_SITE_CWR_000664; IWM_SITE_CWR_000666; IWM_SITE_CWR_000665; IWM_SITE_CWR_000609; MH_531; CWR_002058; IWM_SITE_CWR_000614; Documents_009180_A_1; IWM_SITE_CWR_000111; IWM_SITE_CWR_000612; IWM_SITE_CWR_000613; IWM_SITE_CWR_000598; IWM_SITE_CWR_000672; HU_045346 Courtesy of National Security Agency of the Department of Defence, USA; IWM_SITE_CWR_000670; IWM_SITE_CWR_000671; IWM_SITE_CWR_000673

Chapter 4
NAM_236; HU 55965; IWM_SITE_CWR_000626; IWM_2004_052-0036; HU_103536 © National Portrait Gallery, London; HU_043777; IWM_SITE_CWR_000624; CWR_001825; IWM0018; IWM_SITE_CWR_000625; Documents_009858_A_1; IWM_SITE_CWR_000106; IWM_SITE_CWR_000553; IWM_SITE_CWR_000552; IWM_SITE_CWR_000554; IWM_SITE_CWR_000456; IWM_SITE_CWR_000559; IWM_SITE_CWR_000556; IWM_SITE_CWR_000579; HU_058517; IWM_SITE_CWR_000567; CWR_000406; IWM_SITE_CWR_000575; IWM_SITE_CWR_000573; IWM_SITE_CWR_000570; MAP_DETAIL_1; CWR_000389_1; IWM_SITE_CWR_000674; CWR_001890; HU_074904; CWR_000504; IWM_SITE_CWR_000572; IWM_SITE_CWR_000577; CWR_001842_3; Documents_25644 © Mrs Myra N Collyer (nee Murden); CWR_000788; CWR_001895_1; Documents_002995_C; CWR_001896; CWR_001889_1; CWR_001894

Chapter 5
MH_27624; HeagertyJS_002995_4; IWM_1984_015_120; IWM_SITE_CWR_000362

Index

Page references in *italics* refer to illustrations